DON'T CRY FOR ME

By the same author

Follow My Leader, Kingsway Publications

DON'T CRY FOR ME

Katharine Makower

HODDER AND STOUGHTON
LONDON SYDNEY AUCKLAND TORONTO

British Library Cataloguing in Publication Data

Makower, Katharine
Don't cry for me.
1. Argentina. Christian missions
I. Title
266'.00982

ISBN 0-340-49963-x

Contents

Foreword

The Gran Chaco, which stretches through four republics in South America, was for centuries an unexplored area. Chaco probably means 'Indian hunting-ground': it has also been popularly known as 'the Green Hell'. It is inhospitable from every angle. It is that part of South America where the hottest temperatures are registered. Not only has it been, historically, the home for many different aggressive Indian tribal peoples, but also for poisonous spiders, scorpions, centipedes and snakes, flying bed bugs, varieties of mosquito that take turns so that at least one is on duty throughout twenty-four hours, jaguars, alligators, piranhas and even toads that spit acid and frogs with teeth!

But the Northern Argentine Chaco has also been the setting for a miracle of transformation. It is this story that is told in the pages of this book. In many ways it is not a spectacular story of incredible heroism and dramatic incidents. But it is one of faithfulness and perseverance and of how the Gospel of Christ has not destroyed Indian tribal culture, but enhanced it bringing fulfilment and hope to a pressurised and marginalised people.

Frequently one reads of anthropologists' criticisms of missionary activity among tribal people. This history records the warm appreciative words of famous anthropologists who welcomed the sensitivity and courage of the early pioneers who through their labours and interposition prevented the destruction of the indigenous people.

In 1984, Bishop Mario Mariño, an Indian of the Mataco tribe from Northern Argentina, visited England. He went to many churches, where his spirituality, simple life style, the reality of his walk with Christ and his evident warmth and joy were a challenge to all he met. This book traces the course of history to that point where people from the Gran Chaco are now our 'partners in the Gospel'.

It needed to be recorded and Katharine Makower has done so skilfully and imaginatively.

Patrick Harris, Bishop of Southwell

Author's note

One of the three missionary groups specifically attacked for their destructive effect on the Indian tribes of South America in Norman Lewis's recent book *The Missionaries* is the South American Mission Society. It is important to realise that this is *not* the South American Missionary Society which features in this story, but a completely separate group – the South American Mission Society which is based in the USA. This, like much else, he fails to make clear. The only reference to the SAMS of this book which I could find is that on p. 160, where Lewis quotes Barbrooke Grubb.

The main thrust of his book concerns the dangers of insensitive missionaries barging in on tribal peoples and destroying their way of life. Despite several instances where I am convinced that Norman Lewis has entirely misunderstood and misrepresented the missionaries, there is probably truth in some of what he says. Zealous young Americans are not always the most sensitive of people, and no doubt harm has been done. But the world needs to be reminded that there are also missionaries who, quietly and faithfully and at considerable cost to themselves have done much good, learning tribal languages when no-one else troubled to do so, standing by tribal peoples who would otherwise have been trampled underfoot in the march of exploitation and 'civilisation', and sharing with them the good news of Jesus Christ and of God's love for them. That is the other side to the story, and it, too, needs to be known.

Other Christian groups including, of course, the Roman Catholic Church, are doing valuable work in South America. Among those from this country working in Argentina now are the Evangelical Union of South America (interdenominational), Echoes of Service (Brethren) and the

United Society for the Propagation of the Gospel (Anglican).

I would like to thank the many people who have helped me with this project – too many to mention each by name. In particular I am grateful to Canon Alfred Leake – much of the material presented here is his. His son, Bishop David Leake, has given much help and encouragement, and David and his wife Rachel were hospitality itself when I visited Argentina in 1987. Lois Cumming has been most generous in allowing me to quote from her excellent manuscript based on her own knowledge of the Amerindian villages, and I am grateful to her and to Anna Jones for permission to use Anna's drawings which originally went with Lois's manuscript.

Bishop Bill Flagg, General Secretary of the South American Missionary Society, has given me much support, as have Bishop Pat Harris, recently Secretary of Partnership for World Mission and now Bishop of Southwell, and the Rev. Maurice Jones.

Finally my thanks to the many Christians involved – British, Argentine and Indian (Amerindian) Argentine – who have allowed me to visit them and take up their time with interviews; and to Juliet Newport of Hodder and Stoughton for her enthusiasm and help.

Katharine Makower

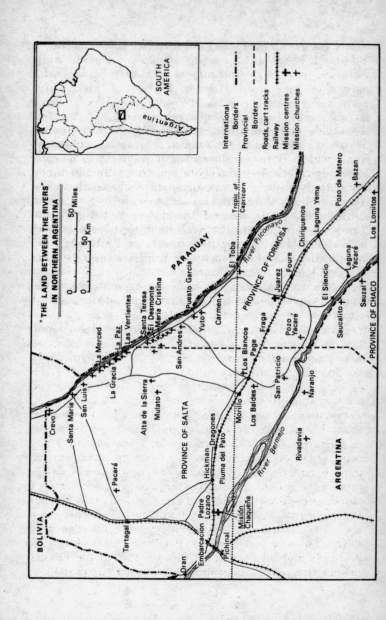

"THE LAND BETWEEN THE RIVERS" IN NORTHERN ARGENTINA

International Borders
Provincial Borders
Roads, cart tracks
Railway
Mission centres
Mission churches

SOUTH AMERICA

Argentina

BOLIVIA

Oran
Tartagal
Embarcacion
Pichinal
Padre Lozano
Misión Chaqueña
Hickman
Dragones
Pluma del Pato
Crevo
Santa Maria
San Luis
Pacará
Alta de la Sierra
Mulato
La Gracia
La Merced
La Paz
Las Vertientes
Santa Teresa
El Desmonte
Maria Cristina
Puesto Garcia
San Andres
Carmen
Yuto
Morillo
Los Baldes
Los Blancos
Page
San Patricio
Naranjo
Rivadavia
Fraga
Pozo Yacaré
San Juarez
El Silencio
El Toba
Foure
Chiriguanos
Laguna Yema
Pozo de Matero
Laguna Yacaré
Saucalito
Sauzal
Los Lomitos
Bazan

PARAGUAY
River Picomayo
Tropic of Capricorn
PROVINCE OF FORMOSA
PROVINCE OF SALTA
PROVINCE OF CHACO
River Bermejo
ARGENTINA

0   50 Miles
0   50 Km

Prologue

I sat in the diocesan office of the Anglican church in Juarez, Northern Argentina. It was August, 1987, and the cold south wind which blows up sometimes in winter was howling round outside. Bishop Mario Mariño, the first Indian bishop in South America, sat informally in front of the desk sipping maté. A short, stocky man in his fifties, he had agreed to answer my questions, and David Leake, the Anglican bishop, was interpreting. Several other men stood around, one replenishing the maté from time to time with hot water and adding alarming quantities of sugar. In one corner Silverio Moreno, Bishop Mario's assistant, was rapping out messages on the radio. The maté passed from one to the other, including David, and each sipped a little through the straw.

'Please make our story known to the brethren in England,' Bishop Mario said. 'We need them to pray for us, then we shan't feel alone. This work is not going to finish, in spite of the difficulties we face.'

'We are glad you have come to meet us for yourself,' another man broke in.

Yes, indeed, I had come to see for myself. For two or three years I had been working on this history, interviewing missionaries in England, reading all I could. Now I had come, at David Leake's invitation, to a country far vaster and more beautiful than I had imagined, and was having the privilege of meeting hundreds of Indian Christians. Some are still raggedly dressed in remote villages; many now manage to look healthy and clean despite the dust everywhere; and some, like these, live in Indian settlements on the edge of the towns. But wherever we went, two things were clear. The gratitude and loyalty felt by these people to the English missionaries are heartfelt; and they still need help to adapt as life changes more and more rapidly around them. It struck me too that as the Lord Jesus Christ himself told mourning onlookers not to weep for him as he went to the cross, so these people could say to us in the words of the song, 'Don't cry for me.' Whilst we may pity the Chaco Indians for their poverty, spiritually they are rich, for they have found the pearl of great price.

I travelled 1,400 miles in ten days along rough, almost deserted roads with David and Rachel Leake. David is the Anglican bishop of Northern Argentina and also Primate of the Southern Cone of South America. Tall, relaxed and young looking despite his white hair, he was born and brought up among the Toba Indians on the banks of the Pilcomayo river, the son of missionaries there. Speaking fluent Spanish, English, Toba and Mataco, he chats on equal terms with everyone he meets, respecting and finding the right level with them all; above all, he listens. Rachel, his wife, a schoolmaster's daughter from Norfolk, is the same. Almost painfully sensitive to the needs of the Indians, once among them she is engulfed, as one after another comes to talk.

At the end of this book I shall describe my tour, as a way of bringing this account of the Church up to date. In the meantime, just a few more vignettes of the people I met, and their message to us:

Calixto, the Indian who mans the radio at Mision Chaqueña, when asked what would have happened to the Indians if the missionaries had not come, was emphatic: 'There would have been no Indians – they would have been wiped out.'

Bishop Mario again, 'Anthropologists come and want to know what the people eat and what they wear – but we are people like everyone else. God loves us as people. We're not just animals!'

And most moving of all, a very old man in a village where we stopped, whose eyes filled with tears as he remembered people who came to them and shared their lives and brought them good news sixty years ago.

Three quotes:

'Already the attention of the Argentine government has been attracted to a phenomenon which in the history of the republic has no precedent, namely the gradual resuscitation of a dying aboriginal race . . .'

Annual Report of the South American
Missionary Society, 1941

'"Travelling round the Chaco, a man cannot fail to be moved by the silent tragedy of a once healthy beautiful race being slowly destroyed by the effects of contact with modern civilisation."
'So wrote the famous anthropologist, Alfred Metraux, who arrived in the Chaco, like so many people, sceptical of the missionaries and unaware of the acute misery among the Indians. He left the area saying,
'"The only gleam of hope is in the presence of the English missionaries. I am not exaggerating when I say that no more beneficial work is being done for the Argentine nation."'

Quoted by Michael Mainwaring in his second article,
'The forgotten Argentines', Buenos Aires Herald, 1969

'The most important influence in the Mataco culture this century is that of the Anglican Protestant missionaries . . . Through their lasting commitment to the protection and welfare of Mataco society, both on the external front with regard to Indian relations with the national society, and on the internal front in the form of agricultural, medical, educational and pastoral activities, the missionaries have won the Matacos' trust and confidence.'

J. H. Palmer: Thesis, Latin American Studies,
Oxford University, 1977

1
'Now you are my sister'

'I must leave Salta. I must get away somewhere and think it all out.' Helena Oliver sat on the veranda of her parents' comfortable home, sipping coffee and talking with a friend. In many ways she was happy in Salta, the beautiful old Spanish colonial city set like a jewel, surrounded by mountains, in the foothills of the Andes of North-West Argentina. Brought up in a well-to-do family, her father a well-known figure in society who bred polo ponies on his farm outside Salta and owned a town house as well, she had received a good education and a strong Roman Catholic upbringing from her mother in particular, who was very devout. After studying at the University of Cordoba, she had been asked, together with a Jesuit priest from America, to set up a Department of Social Services in the University of Salta. Now in the 1970s this was going well, with a good team of dedicated people working in the poor parts of the town and exploring new methods and theories of social development.

None the less she was uneasy. She felt she was leading a double life, concerned about the poor, but living well herself. The situation was becoming unbearable to her – having so much, living in this rich and beautiful part of the city and theorising day after day to bright, prosperous, well-dressed students like herself, while the other half of Argentine society, powerless and largely helpless, was kept out of sight and where possible out of mind. Feeling that somehow she must resolve her own confusion, she had begged a year's leave of absence from the university to get away and think the problem out – a quiet place somewhere, among simple people – but where? Somewhere in the mountains, perhaps?

'What about the Chaco?' suggested her friend. Helena thought. She had read about the Gran Chaco, but although it was not far away, she had never been there. It was certainly not a place one would choose for a holiday. By all accounts it included some of the flattest, most monotonous countryside imaginable. The twenty thousand of the country's remaining Indians lived there, on land that hardly anyone else wanted as extremes of drought and flooding made it hard to cultivate. Many Argentinians knew nothing of these aboriginals, or *indigenas*, but Helena knew that primitive Indian tribes still lived there, in small settlements mostly on the river banks.

'I know just the place for you,' her friend insisted. He was an anthropologist and director of the government department concerned with the aboriginals. 'There's a government project planned for Santa Maria, a village on the River Pilcomayo where both *Criollos* [Argentine settlers] and Indians live. We need someone to work on this project, but no one wants to go. You must go, Helena; it's just the place for you.'

Yes! She would go – at any rate to see. But it was midsummer: the wet season and the roads would be very bad. 'How to get there?' she wondered. 'I could take the train to Tartagal, but what to do after that?'

Her resourceful friend had the answer yet again: 'Go to the Anglican people. They have tractors. They can get you through.' So, never one to linger once she had made up her mind, Helena packed a few belongings and off she went.

In Tartagal she found someone from the Anglican mission at the riverside village of La Paz who had come in with the tractor to collect supplies, and begged a lift from him. Bumping along the rutted mud-swamped road between the tall trees and tangled undergrowth, she surveyed her fellow passengers with a certain feeling of superiority. One of them appeared to be reading a Bible as they went along. 'Funny gringo!' was Helena's comment to herself. 'What kind of people are these?' They were kind, though. They seemed to have quite a big team at La Paz, and they welcomed her and gave her food and a bed. Next day Mary Dibb, a nurse, took her over to Santa Maria and introduced her to the people, speaking to them – and here Helena was impressed – in their own language – Mataco:

'This is Helena. She is hoping to come here to work on a government programme for helping you and building better houses. Please welcome her.'

The Indians conferred together for some time and then one of them spoke.

'We are tired of people coming with all these programmes. They come by car and truck and give us empty promises and go away again. If Helena wants to come, she must *live* with us and she must *believe* in us – these two things.'

For Helena, that settled it. 'These were people who knew what they wanted. I could be happy with them.'

As soon as she could, therefore, she came back to Santa Maria in a government jeep. The journey took three days because of the mud. The government had built a house for the project worker in the part of the village where the *Criollos* lived. It had a shower, a toilet, a Calor-gas fire and a pump. For the first night Helena lived there most comfortably, but the next day the Indians appeared. She didn't yet speak a word of Mataco, but they made their meaning plain enough in Spanish.

'So you came, Helena. But what are you doing here? We agreed that you would come and live with us!'

They picked up her tent and her rucksack without more ado, and took her to their part of the village. The dogs, yapping with excitement, came running out, and so did the children, to see the young woman with her long black plait of hair and her eager, intense face framed with bright earrings. In no time they put her tent up near the church, and gave her a bed which Zebedeo, the pastor, had made for her and also a chair. Later they helped her with building a house just like theirs, and she settled down truly to live with them, going barefoot as they did, going with the women to fetch water and wood.

Vivacious and enthusiastic, always eager to learn, she soon made friends among the villagers, both children and adults, and from them began to pick up the Mataco

Women filling their water-pots from the river – the Pilcomayo at La Paz.

language. She soon found she would have no peace and quiet; if privacy for meditation was what she wanted, she would not find much opportunity for it here. However, twice a day, morning and evening, a piece of old iron outside the church was banged by way of a bell, and the villagers would leave what they were doing and go into the church. Helena, wanting to identify with them as completely as possible, went too. The service wasn't quiet – far from it. As well as adults, there were children of all ages, dogs and even the occasional hen. The singing was enthusiastic, but not always tuneful. It was far from the beautifully ordered worship which Helena had known from her childhood. What was more, it didn't even seem to be an established Roman Catholic church.

Strangely though, as Helena sat with her new friends day by day, or listened as Zebedeo, his face lit up, explained the Scriptures in vivid picture language, she began to feel that here, among some of the most neglected people on earth, she was finding the light that had eluded her in her privileged, sophisticated town life until now. And this light seemed to be inextricably linked with a person who was clearly a living reality to the people around her – the Light of the World, Jesus Christ.

For many months Helena lived among her new friends, listening, learning the language, wondering. She recalls how 'One Indian, an older man and an elder in the church, called Silvo Perez, impressed me particularly. He and others were very concerned about some married couples in the village who seemed to have difficulties and were in danger of separating. Sometimes, in the afternoons, Silvo and others would go and visit these people and try to help them, and I would go too.

'For a while everyone talked a bit and asked about the problem. Time didn't seem to matter. Then after a long time Silvo Perez would begin to talk, meditatively and persuasively. He began from the Creation, I remember, and told how God formed man from the dust of the ground. The man had no life, but God breathed life. But the man was alone, and God saw that this wasn't good, so he made woman from the rib of the man, so that Adam could rejoice, "This at last is bone of my bone and flesh of my flesh" – therefore a man leaves his father and mother and cleaves to his wife.

'From here Silvo Perez went through the Bible, telling the people of God's loving plan of salvation. I was amazed. He did all this without reading from the Bible at all – he couldn't read. Who had taught him? Certainly the missionaries had, but I know now that God's Holy Spirit had been his teacher, too.

'I had had a good Roman Catholic upbringing. I knew about Jesus and it was right what I had been taught, but these Pilcomayo people seemed to *know* him for themselves, and they brought me to know his love, too. In my enthusiasm and ignorance I used to say to them, "When I die, I want to be put in the earth as you do it, without a coffin, with all of you here." But Zebedeo, gently as always, corrected me.

'"Helena, you always say you will be with us for ever. I have to tell you that we love you a lot and you love us, but this love is something which will end. Long ago, God spared his people, the Jews, from destruction, telling them to kill the Passover lamb and mark their doorposts with its blood; now after many years, God sent his Son to us. He died on the Cross. Now God promises us that everyone who believes in Jesus will have the mark of the blood of Jesus in his heart and he, too, will be saved and forgiven. This love, Helena, never ends. When we die, the worms eat our bodies [this I saw], but if we believe in Jesus we have eternal life and go to be with him for ever.'

'It was so clear, but I found it hard to accept. For about two years the people of Santa Maria had been showing me God's love – not only in words, but in their actions. I believed and trusted everything they said. Slowly I began to see that I must also accept this truth from them.'

Finally, one day when a baptism was planned, a group of the older men in Santa Maria came to see her. 'Helena,' Zebedeo said as their spokesman, 'we have something to say to you. We are glad that you have been living with us and as one of us. We have come to love you as a daughter. But in the most important thing we feel we are not yet one. We urge you to turn to our Saviour Jesus Christ and to be baptised in his name with the others tomorrow.'

Helena looked at them, wondering: 'Oh my friends – what can I say? I have been baptised. It is our way to baptise people as very small babies. My mother would be very distressed if I decided to be baptised again.' She hesitated. 'Please give me time to think, and come back to me after this evening's service.'

Quickly, before the bell rang, she ran to the church, and knelt there on the dusty floor in the half-darkness. What should she do? She had come to understand for the first time from Zebedeo's simple preaching that Jesus had died on the Cross to bear the burden and penalty of all that she, Helena, was. She must bring to him the burden of all her and her people's arrogance and complacency. If she did this, in some mysterious way she would become washed and clean. And what better could symbolise this cleansing than baptism? Yes, she would be baptised by her Indian friends as a symbol, sincere, though confused theologically, of her identification with the Indian people among whom she had found Christ as a living reality. As she knelt, she asked Christ into her life and became, as he promised, a new creation. Her inner conflict seemed to resolve itself and she wept tears of gratitude and peace.

The next day Helena was baptised, along with the other new believers. As she left the church, Zebedeo took her hand and gave her a loving welcome: 'You are now no longer my daughter, Helena, you are my sister in Christ.'

And so Helena with all her advantages found the answers to her questions through a rejected group of tribal people living in the forest. What lay behind this story, and how these remote Indians came to learn the good news which met Helena's need, is what the rest of this book is about.

2
The Franciscans' Prayer

Both the Jesuits and the Franciscans had worked with much
love and dedication to bring Christianity to the Indians of
this area many years before. Early in the seventeenth century
a Jesuit priest, Gaspar Osorio, visited a group of Toba
Indians to the north of Salta and began teaching them; he
was later killed by Chiriguano Indians, becoming, as the
historian Father Corrado commented, 'the first apostle
whose blood was spilt on the arid Chaco soil.'[1] This work
among the Tobas inhabiting the West of the Chaco was
continued against heavy odds by the Jesuits until their
expulsion from the Spanish colonies by order of King Charles
III of Spain in 1767. It was then taken over by Franciscans
from Jujuy who found the Tobas very fickle, but eventually,
through much patient work, led some of them to faith. Later
the mission here was ransacked by a local military despot
who drove the Indians away with bullets and settled with his
troops on the mission, turning the church into a sugar store
and the vestry into a wine store, using the altar for grinding
aji – dwarf red peppers – and up-ending the bells and using
them as cauldrons. As Father Corrado remarked, 'the hand
trembles at the thought of the horrors which were per-
petrated, not by a horde of savage Indians, but by spurious
Christians.'

When the Jesuits had to leave, Franciscans also came
down from their convent at Tarija, in Bolivia, to set up
missions among the Mataco Indians – notably Mision Zenta,
which was established in 1779 about a hundred miles north
of Salta near the River Bermejo. (Very near this same spot,
the first Anglican mission in the Argentine Chaco was set up
135 years later – Mision Chaqueña, at Algarrobal.) The
Indians of this district had asked the priests at Tarija for a

mission, and their petition was supported by the governor of the province of Salta who thought it would impede the frequent invasions of the wild frontier Indians. For this reason, as Father Corrado observed, 'it cost much and accomplished little.'

Two priests from Tarija were chosen for this work, and they were allotted twenty-four soldiers for protection. Between them, priests and soldiers gradually built a protective enclosure, or fort, and a large house and chapel. Later they planted large walled gardens and orchards, but they had little success. The Indians came and settled on the site, building themselves crude shelters of branches; they seemed to the priests to be aggressive, slovenly and unresponsive. It was said that when the bell was rung for prayer, the Indians would either hide themselves or flee to the forest, and that when a missionary was trying to help or to heal one of them, they would just watch stolidly, seemingly without any response or sense of gratitude.

In particular, the building of the city of Nueva Oran near to Mision Zenta in 1794 unsettled the Indians and gradually undid all the work of the mission, so that in the end it had to be abandoned. The missionaries had been tireless in their efforts, but the Matacos failed to respond. And as Father Corrado commented sadly, 'If the Indians did not take advantage of this, if they did not listen, did not attend and did not stay permanently on the mission, what more could they do? The Indians profited little or nothing, but the missionaries gained much, for they knew how to bear the burdens, discomforts, and vexations, with patience and resignation to the will of God.'

There was much intertribal fighting, and the Indians showed little trust for the missionaries either – possibly because they found it hard to distinguish between them and the colonial power who, after all, spoke the same language – Spanish – and who were misleadingly often known by the same name – Cristianos. Later, when 'white people from over the sea' came specially to help them, 'speaking their words', as they put it, they were better able to respond.

The Franciscans from Tarija also attempted work among the Tobas, whom they describe as a fierce tribe who wandered over the open grasslands between the Bermejo and Pilcomayo rivers, assaulting, pillaging and killing. According to Father Corrado, 'from time immemorial they had played havoc in their relations with their neighbours – always keeping them on tenterhooks, wondering what they would do next, for their behaviour was quite unpredictable. Today they would be dancing and drinking with them as the greatest of friends – tomorrow fighting and chopping off their heads in careless abandon.'

He recounts how the Spanish conquistadores became a threat to the Tobas when they began advancing into their territory. In earlier years their concern was for a route through from the Paraguay River to the wealth of Peru. Later it was for the preservation of their national boundaries. Whatever the reason for their presence, the stealthy encroachment of the military infuriated the Tobas, and they gathered together the Matacos and rose in rebellion with them against the intruders. 'With the cunning of the fox and the ferocity of the jaguar,' Father Corrado tells us, 'they launched themselves against the "white" colonies of Esteco, Salta, and Jujuy, killing men, stealing cattle, and devastating populations.' He comments, too, on the peaceful attempts of 'conquistadores' of another kind – the Franciscans – even though, as he says, there were few happy results of their efforts to 'bend the inflexible necks of the proud Tobas to the yoke of Christ by persuasion!'

As the history records, 'Often the situation seemed hopeless, but there were rays of light, as on July 24th, 1860, when "the sun shone again", as two Franciscan missionaries could be seen carrying a roughly-hewn wooden cross along the bed of the upper reaches of the River Pilcomayo, surrounded by a silent wondering crowd of Tobas.' When this cross was erected, all those assembled – priests, Chiriguanos and their age-old enemies the Tobas – came forward in pairs to kiss the cross, after which the two priests put on their robes and held a solemn service of exorcism so that all demons should vacate the place where the new mission was to be built. That was the start of the mission of San Francisco – on the northern reaches of the Pilcomayo in Bolivia. Apparently the Tobas rallied round with enthusiasm, showing a real desire to work, building houses and gardens and displaying great affection and respect for the missionaries. Yet, in spite of all the hopeful signs, the enterprise failed.

What happened was this: in the year 1862, the harvest being very poor, many of the resident Indians were forced to leave San Francisco and go searching for food. When the news of the depleted numbers at the mission reached the ears of some non-mission Indians living near by, they decided that this was the time to strike and get rid of the missionaries. For some reason, there was only one missionary resident at the time; he was completely without any defence, and it would be easy to kill him, to pillage the mission and set fire to the buildings. During the afternoon of October 4th, a combined horde of three to four hundred Indians headed towards San Francisco. When news of this invading force reached the mission there was great consternation as there were only about twenty men there altogether, of whom only four could use firearms. They did all they could to prepare for the expected attack, and the missionary removed everything valuable from the church, distributed the guns and ammunition, tried to console and encourage the Indians, and committed himself to God.

The day of October 5th, 1862, had scarcely dawned when those at the mission saw that the bed of the river seemed to be covered by warlike men. As they watched, they saw about seven of them leave the main group and begin to walk in the direction of the mission. At the same time, another seven men on horses and carrying firebrands also made their way to the mission with the intention of setting it on fire, and those on foot, carrying axes and stakes, followed them to tear down the buildings. So the conflict began. Lances and stones rained down into the fort, two arrows pierced the lintels of the tower where the missionary had taken refuge, and there seemed little hope for him and the handful of defenders. But something very strange was happening, for the main force in the river-bed was making no attempt to follow up the vanguard in the attack! Had they done so, the mission and all its occupants would have been doomed, for as the author says, 'What could twenty defenders do against a horde of four hundred?' He asks, 'Who kept them standing transfixed in the river-bed?' and affirms that he has no fear in saying that it was 'a hand invisible'.

The combat lasted for barely half an hour, because the fourteen attackers, for no known reason, suddenly turned their backs and fled, leaving trails of blood in their wake. The horde in the river-bed, seeing what had happened, all disappeared into the forest as quickly and quietly as they had appeared in the early dawn. At the mission there was stunned surprise and relief; only two people had been slightly wounded and none had been killed. Some buildings had been burnt, but the church, despite its thatched roof, was unharmed. There missionary and Indians together thanked God for their deliverance.

More trouble was in the wind, however, with the building by the military of a fort near-by at Bella Esperanza, as part of the gradual colonisation of the Chaco from Caixa to the Pilcomayo, and its sacking on September 13th, 1867, by non-mission Tobas. During this, and another dramatic attack on a military expedition heading for Paraguay, the mission Tobas remained faithful to the 'whites', with the result that the Tobas from outside decided once again to destroy the mission. On the night of January 19th, 1869, when all at the mission were peacefully sleeping, the attack came. A mixed crowd of Tobas and others had come up quietly and penetrated to the centre of the group of Toba huts, where they began shooting arrows at the sleeping Indians. As the wounded cried out, the Tobas and Chiriguanos living on the mission, 'fleet of foot as deer', jumped out of their hammocks and hurled themselves on the invaders with such force that they lost their courage and fled. The defenders chased them for quite a way, and the heads of three of the dead insurgents were brought back, thrown around and rolled in the mud. That day, apparently, 'they served as a barbarous diversion for the children' and finally were hung up in a tree where they stayed for many months as symbols of the victory.

The mission had indeed come through another crisis victoriously, but although many Chiriguanos became faithful Christians, there was little spiritual progress among the Tobas at San Francisco. They loved wandering, and even travelled as far as Oran, where their contact with the 'cristianos' (white men), which should have influenced them for good, encouraged them in drunkenness and prostitution, and generally demoralised them. Particularly affected in this way was an insolent Toba named Cusurai, whom they taught to use firearms, trying, as Father Corrado sadly puts it, 'to domesticate the young lion by sharpening his claws'. This Cusurai became more and more arrogant and difficult, and finally left the mission altogether on the night of September 27th, 1873, taking several families with him. From then onwards, from his haunt in the deep forest of Teyu, he tried to encourage rebellion among the mission Tobas who, however, resisted him and remained loyal to the padre until one night when a rumour reached the mission that Cusurai, with a large group of Tobas, was camping not far away. This proved to be true when some messengers from Cusurai crept silently into the Toba village. What news did they bring? No one knows, but the result of the visit was obvious the following morning when the sun rose, for the huts of all the Tobas were empty. They had finally left the mission.

This was a sad ending to the years of effort which had been put into bringing the Gospel to these northern Tobas, for, as Father Corrado put it, 'The Cross had extended its arms in vain to bless them.' In order to preserve the mission of San Francisco, and to protect it from further attacks, 380 Chiriguanos from Tarairi moved on to the site, and among them the Gospel took root.

Then followed more turbulent months, with the Tobas and several other Indian tribes stirring each other up to a fierce determination not only to destroy the missions of San

Francisco and San Antonio on the other side of the river, but also to clear their ancestors' territory of all 'whites', who were gradually occupying the region. After many bloody battles, the governor of the district ordered the building of a fort, and

> in February 1875 all the forces made up of soldiers and loyal Indians were united in the valley of Caipeperenda and there, after destroying many families, they tumultuously killed sixty Chiriguanos and Cheneses before the eyes of their mothers and wives who, filling the air with their wailing, were made captive and taken away. This frightful slaughter terrified the leaders of the revolt and they, with their people, fled to the most impenetrable forests and to the jungles of the lower Pilcomayo.

In August 1879 the remaining mission Indians fled, and finally the Franciscans decided to pull out altogether. That was in 1882 after two massacres. First Jules Crévaux, a well-known Frenchman who was exploring the Pilcomayo to see if it could be made navigable, and fourteen men with him, were murdered by Tobas; and a few months later the same thing happened to an expedition organised by the Bolivian government. The place where Crévaux was killed was named after him, and is not many miles upstream from Santa Maria where Helena Oliver came to live almost a hundred years later. The Franciscans gave up after that, and left, leaving their lovely buildings to crumble. But they committed the continuation of their work to God, and the historian of their dedicated efforts finished his book with these words:

> With an aching heart we lay aside our pen, lifting up humble and ardent supplication to the Father of all, that he may have compassion on his unhappy children of the Pilcomayo and, at last, cause to shine on them the Sun of truth and grace, enlightening them and giving them peace.

This prayer was to be answered in unexpected ways.

3
Early Days

In 1846 while the Franciscans were struggling with great dedication and patience to bring the Gospel of peace to the Indians, an Englishman visited the Chaco. A captain in the Royal Navy, Allen Gardiner had become conscious of the spiritual need of the South American Indians when he had called at various South American ports quite early in his naval career. He observed how they hated and feared the settlers, and how too, apart from the isolated efforts of the Franciscans, the established Roman Catholic church had little time for them. He felt so strongly that something should be done, that back in England he tried to persuade the London Missionary Society to start work in South America, and even offered to go himself, at his own expense, as a member of the missionary team. His offer was turned down, and, on the death of his wife, he turned his attention and energy to South Africa.

After some years spent establishing relations with the fierce King Dingaan in the hopes of taking the Gospel to the Zulus – and founding the city of Durban in the process – he visited South America again, on his way home to England, and this time his second wife and children were with him. Wherever they asked about the possibility of work among the Indian tribes they were discouraged, and their travels across the Andes and into Chile fared no better. They met with Indian chiefs who were friendly, but such was the fear of the white man, that none dared invite them to stay.

Next, from a base in the Falkland Islands, Allen Gardiner visited Patagonia, in the south of South America, and from here he wrote, firstly to the Church Missionary Society and then to the London Missionary Society, appealing to them to found a mission in Patagonia. Neither at that time had the resources to enable them to take up the challenge, so back in England in 1844 he founded a very small society – the Patagonian Mission. After a short and not very successful stay among the Indian tribes of Patagonia, Gardiner decided to visit the Gran Chaco. He and a young Spaniard, Miguel Gonzalez, set off from Liverpool in September 1845 and spent six months in the Bolivian Chaco, visiting Mataco and Chiriguano Indians. Sadly, in spite of his prayer, 'Thou knowest, Lord . . . that tomorrow in all probability a final answer will be given respecting our admittance into the Chiriguano country. Whatever it may be, I know that it will be exactly that which is known and purposed by Thee,'[2] his request to buy a plot of land and settle among them was refused by the Chiriguano chief, zealous to preserve the rights of his people to their ancestral land. The Matacos had indicated that they would be willing, if only the Chiriguanos agreed. They did not; but they were impressed by him. At one point Gardiner hired an Indian to swim across the Pilcomayo with him: 'Away we went, leaning together on a bundle of reeds. The current was full four or five knots, but we gained the opposite side in good style, the Indians all aghast to see a white man who could swim as well as themselves.'

A plan of Gardiner's to buy some land from the Bolivian Government, on which Indians could live and work and receive instruction in the Christian faith, was discouraged by the British Consul in La Paz. The present Bolivian Government, he conceded, was broad-minded and tolerant, and might agree to it, but the ecclesiastical hierarchy – that was a different matter! In the end, limited permission was given, which resulted in Gonzalez settling in the small town of Potosi with freedom to learn the language of the local Quechua tribes and to start visiting and evangelising among them. It was a start, and soon another young Spanish Protestant was sent out to join him. Gardiner, meanwhile, went back to England to report to his society. At first they were doubtful about taking on this ambitious work themselves, and approached the Church Missionary Society who were again unable to commit themselves. Slowly Gardiner attracted enthusiastic supporters to the Patagonian Mission, and from then onwards, his own efforts were concentrated on the Indians who lived on the bleak islands at the very tip of South America – Tierra del Fuego – and there, in the Antarctic winter of 1851 he and six others died on the beach at Spaniard Harbour, where they had been waiting six months for supplies.[3] In a last prayer found in his diary near his body, he had asked: 'Let not this mission fail, though we should not be permitted to labour in it, but graciously raise up other labourers, who may convey the saving truths of Thy Gospel to the poor blind heathen around us . . .'

This tragic ending could be seen as the final failure of all Allen Gardiner's hopes and dreams. In fact it proved to be the beginning. While *The Times* deplored the wastage of lives and money on hordes of savages at the other side of the world when so much need cried out to be met at home, many others were deeply moved by the heroism of Gardiner and his friends. The upsurge of emotion was nationwide with poems being written in their honour, and the small Patagonian Mission was inspired to declare, 'This is not the end – with God's help, the Mission shall go on.' And so it did. Later, in 1864, it became known as the South American Missionary Society (SAMS).

Over the next few years, starting from Keppel Island of the Falklands, missionaries began work not only in Tierra del Fuego but among the Araucanians and Mapuches of Southern Chile and in Patagonia. In 1863 the small missionary team on Keppel Island was joined by a young clergyman, Waite Stirling, who after six years' hard work, which included seven months solitary witness as 'God's sentinel, stationed at the southernmost outpost of his great army'[4] at Ushaia on Beagle Channel, Tierra del Fuego, was appointed Anglican Bishop of the Falkland Islands and South America. As such he was given responsibility not only wherever SAMS missionaries were at work, but also for any British chaplains throughout South America and their congregations. He was enthroned on January 14th, 1872, in the public building known as St Thomas's Church, Stanley – in fact it had been built as the corn exchange.

Bishop Stirling's new work was not easy, as the chaplains resident in the various republics of South America had been licensed by the Bishop of London, and were not at first keen to transfer their allegiance. Most of these were consular chaplains; some were chaplains to trading or mining communities. Gradually his dedication and kindly personality won them over. He set high standards for his chaplains, too, and insisted that the good news of Jesus Christ must be shared with everyone, regardless of class or race. Writing for example about a possible candidate to a chaplaincy:

> . . . I told him I could scarcely be induced to give him a Licence if I did not think he would do all in his power to make Christ known to the black slave population; that I did not ask him to attempt to proselytise the slaves who are nominally Roman Catholic; but that I could not bear to think of his being a chaplain to a slave-working company, without doing all in his power to bring the law of Christ to bear upon master and slave, to the good of all. Not to be a missionary in such circumstances, but merely a chaplain to the ruling few, would be heartless indeed. We go to the English and come in contact with the African, or the Indian, or emigrants from China, and so on. But if our chaplains take pains to limit their work, and hedge it off, our opportunities perish.[5]

One such opportunity presented itself in 1886, with the arrival in South America of a remarkable man – Barbrooke Grubb.

4
The Livingstone of South America

Wilfred Barbrooke Grubb was not a chaplain, in fact, but came out to work among the Indians as a missionary. He was brought up in a devout and comfortably-off Scottish family, his father a doctor. Brave and physically strong, from childhood he had loved stories of adventure and travel. When he was about 19, he felt God calling him to missionary work, and applied to the South American Missionary Society. In the course of his interview with them, the chairman, referring to the death of Allen Gardiner, solemnly asked the young candidate if he wanted to be a martyr: 'No, sir, I do not,' was the equally solemn reply. He was accepted and sailed out in March 1886.

He had hoped to be appointed at once to pioneer work among the Indians, but Bishop Stirling had other ideas: 'You are a soldier of Christ; you must not pick and choose, but go where you are sent.' So for three years he was sent to work and train at Keppel. It didn't take Stirling long, though, to recognise his potential, and he commented to a friend, 'If that young man lives, he will become the Livingstone of South America!' And that indeed proved to be the case. At last in 1889 the call came in the form of a telegram from the bishop, 'Send Grubb Paraguay', and off he went.

Paraguay and Bolivia are the only two republics of South America without a coastline, and as one looks at the map, Paraguay is to be seen nestling in the very heart of the continent, divided in two by the River Paraguay which flows southwards to its confluence with the Parana and eventually the River Plate at Buenos Aires. Grubb commented, in his fascinating book, *An Unknown People in an Unknown Land*, how strange it was that,

with only a few miles dividing them, you see on the one
[Western] bank of the river primitive man as he was
centuries ago, and on the other the highly cultivated
European, both equally ignorant of the life of the other. It
seems almost incredible that, for nearly four generations,
civilisation and Christianity have sat facing barbarism
and heathenism, and yet have stood wholly apart.[6]

He comments, too, on the physical differences between the
two halves of the country: the eastern half undulating,
pleasant, easy to cultivate; to the west 'an almost dead-level
plain, covering an area of two hundred thousand square
miles, and consisting of alluvial mud swept down in past ages
from the foothills of the Andes. Not a pebble or stone can
be found, and it is often in flood time almost converted
into a great shallow lake.'[7] Here Grubb is describing the
Paraguayan Chaco, and as somebody once warned him
before he went there, 'The Chaco has the form of a saucer and
once the river overflows its banks you will be drowned like
rats.'

It was in Paraguay that the Jesuits in the seventeenth and
eighteenth centuries had achieved among the Guarani what
Voltaire described as the triumph of humanity, holding sway
among the Indians in a benevolent Christian 'colony' for a
century and a half. But that was not in the Chaco. Needless to
say, it was the Chaco, the agelong home of the unknown
people in the unknown land, that interested Grubb.

Paraguay at this time was only just beginning to recover
from the devastation of the five-year war under Marshal
Lopez against the united forces of Brazil, Argentina and
Uruguay, and had recently become a free republic after years
of despotism. The land to the west of the river was quite
unexplored, and was being sold off to speculators by the
government, who simply marked off the River Paraguay into
sections, drew imaginary lines westwards to the River Pilcomayo, and let the new owners, who had often never even seen
the land, make the best of it.

A mission to the Indians of Paraguay had been urged upon

Bishop Stirling by Dr Stewart, the British Consul in Asuncion, and also by Admiral Sulivan. The latter had sailed with Charles Darwin, as second lieutenant on the *Beagle* some years earlier, and was a keen supporter of missions, and of the South American Missionary Society in particular. Like Allen Gardiner, he had become conscious of the needs of the unevangelised tribes while serving on the River Parana. This work was started, with the encouragement of the Paraguayan Government, by Mr Adolfo Henriksen, an agent of the British and Foreign Bible Society, and shortly after Henriksen's death Barbrooke Grubb arrived to take over the work. He reached Riacho Fernandez, a small mission station which Hendriksen had established on land belonging to the Anglo-Paraguayan Land Company about thirty miles upstream of Concepcion, in 1889.

Grubb settled down well, and was soon on good terms with the river-bank Indians, but he was eager to move westwards and to go and live among the tribes of the interior, a thing which no white person had yet done and lived to tell the tale. He felt it was important for missionaries to reach them before the settlers did, who always seemed to corrupt them. His idea was to visit and to live for short spells periodically with the Indians, 'in order to master their language, understand their customs, win their confidence, and obtain influence over them for good.' Eventually, after careful planning and preparation, on September 9th, 1890, with three Indian guides, an Englishman as companion, eight horses and a month's supplies, he left the bank of the Paraguay and set off westwards. He was to travel miles, sometimes drenched in torrential rain, sometimes despairing of finding water, always pursued by myriads of insects.

It is not my task to write about his adventures. This has been done fully in his own books and in Richard Hunt's biography, *The Livingstone of South America*. Suffice it to say that Barbrooke Grubb, vigorous, dedicated, tough, with all the qualities of leadership needed for a pioneer, acquired over the next twenty years an unparalleled knowledge of the beliefs and customs of the Indian tribes among whom he lived. He really did share their lives, often sitting among them and sharing their pipe as it was passed round; listening as they told their tales. Once at least his labours nearly cost him his life when an Indian who had a guilty conscience in connection with some cattle he had stolen, fearing discovery shot Grubb in the back with a steel-tipped arrow which almost pierced his lungs.

The Indians of the Paraguayan Chaco were nomadic, living in the roughest of shelters, prone to abandon a settlement at the slightest provocation – outbreak of illness, shortage of food, or fear of evil spirits. The spirits of the dead frightened them particularly, so that after a death, the village where it occurred would be burnt and abandoned. As the Christian message began to be understood and accepted, these fears were allayed and a more settled life style emerged.

Gradually a few missionary colleagues joined Grubb – notably Richard Hunt and Andrew Pride, and mission stations were established, including Waikthlatingmangyalwa – the central station which was built on land which had been given to the mission by the government. The surveyor who measured out the land reported to the government, 'I am surprised at the security and tranquillity with which we can now travel among the Chaco Indians, thanks to the effective measures taken by the missionaries to Christianise these savages.'[8]

Some indeed were truly converted, and in 1898 a church was built and soon the first two converts were baptised. With the beginning of the new century some missionaries with industrial experience joined the team, and the Paraguayan Chaco Indian Association was set up, which provided work and industrial training for the Indians. A cattle ranch was established where the Indians were taught to work as cowboys, and later a garden settlement on a fertile island in the swamp at Makthlawaiya, a place to which in 1908 the central mission station was transferred.

Grubb was always conscious that the missionary must 'get rid as soon as possible of his narrow, conservative and self-satisfied insular ideas. His object is to win men for Christ

and not to make them Englishmen.' Thus he never encouraged the Indians to change their (scanty) mode of dress.
None the less, it was inevitable that with the coming of the
Gospel their hand-to-mouth way of life would change. Grubb
was convinced that 'It is a mistake to think that the Indian is
contented and happy in his miserable and degraded state;
the truth is rather that he has discovered no way of altering
it.' This Grubb and his colleagues worked hard to help the
Indians to do, and it is fascinating to read of the innovations
they introduced. When they arrived, the people had no
notion of the different days of the week. As Grubb observed,
'We had no difficulty in inculcating the observance of
Sunday; there was more difficulty in persuading people to
observe the six days of toil!'

Hard work, co-operation, thrift – even a native police force
whose members were so proud of their uniforms that they
were loth to remove them at night! Some of these changes
might seem regrettable to us now, with our consciousness of
the value of the old tribal ways. But these were doomed
anyway – the settlers were buying up the land. Grubb was
recognised with gratitude by the Paraguayan Government as
the '*Pacificador de los Indios*', but he was never one to rest on his
laurels. By 1910 his mind was probing northwards and
westwards, where the rest of the Chaco lay under its green
forest covering, the people who lived in its remote settlements
still a prey to superstition and fear.

As he pondered, it seemed to him that the best way to
reach them was not to push on westwards from where he was
until he reached the distant Pilcomayo on its eastern (Paraguayan) bank, but to approach the Argentine Chaco from
the comparative civilisation of the north-west. He was particularly eager to reach a remote and reputedly dangerous
tribe, the Tobas, the same people who farther north and in
the previous century had proved too much for the Franciscans and who quite recently had been involved in attacks on,
and consequent punitive forays by the Argentinian authorities. When he heard that large numbers of Indians were
being currently employed in the sugar plantations of

northern Argentina, he wondered whether this might be the place to begin. Here at last, he felt, might be the motive of self-interest 'stepping in to lead the Government to protect and legalise the aboriginals, rather than trying to exterminate and control them by military force'.

So, in 1910, after leave in England and consultation with the SAMS committee, he visited the Leach brothers – the English family who owned and ran one of the biggest sugar plantations, La Esperanza, at a place called San Pedro, between Salta and Embarcacion. The meeting was mutually satisfactory, and on his return from a journey farther north-wards to Santa Cruz in Bolivia, Grubb received a letter from the Leaches, expressing warm sympathy for his idea of starting a mission on their estate, and offering him a house and use of a portion of their land for no rent.

He arrived on April 11th, 1911, and with him a small party of pioneers from Paraguay. Here were spent three useful years, during which the missionaries established friendly relations with members of the various local tribes, and Richard Hunt in particular, a gifted linguist, made consider-able headway with their languages. He described their progress in these words:

To old Geronimo must be given the credit of recognising in us friends and fellow 'Indians' . . . one day he turned to me, in a serious and solemn manner that demanded attention and said, 'Tell me, sir, why do you take such an interest in us, and ignore the Argentines? Why do you want to write down our words, and make enquiries about our customs and early history? You tell me that you have lived for a long time among other Indians, and I realise that you speak truly, for you are different to the ordinary traveller, or even the English owners of this place, though they are good.' People gathered round, and without realis-ing what I was doing, I was soon launched into my first Spanish sermon. Possibly for an hour, in simple language, I told them about God, and the Creation, and the coming of our Lord. To my surprise, the audience sat spellbound. I made rapid progress in the Vejoz [a form of Mataco] language, and in the first seventeen days had collected a vocabulary of some two thousand words, and in addition had thought out and verified the main grammatical points.

This shows something of Richard Hunt's remarkable ability with languages. In a short time he had reduced Mataco to order and had written it down.

Grubb's hope, though, was to establish a mission station where the Indians could live, rather than merely to meet them transiently at their place of work. He had more ambitious hopes, too, of a line of mission stations across the Gran Chaco. This proved impossible because of the shortage of men caused by the Great War, but nonetheless on December 4th, 1914, shortly after the outbreak of the First World War, he and his small mission party arrived at Algarrobal, an estate which he had bought for the mission near the railway terminus of Embarcacion; and there Mision Chaqueña (the Chaco mission) began.

5
An Irish Boy

In April 1912, while Barbrooke Grubb and his colleagues were living among the Indian sugar-cane workers at San Pedro, an Irish boy of 13, who curiously enough bore the same surname but was not a relation, was blithely setting off on his first holiday abroad, as he announced in his beautifully kept diary. His name was Henry Grubb, and this was to be the first of many journals which he kept meticulously, and the first of many journeys which he made.

His home was the family estate in Ireland: Ardmayle, Cashel, Tipperary, where his childhood was privileged, happy and secure. His father was a Deputy Lieutenant and widely respected in the county; the family were staunch members of the Church of Ireland. Henry was the eldest child, and there was always plenty to do at home, with their many friends and relations and his two brothers and little sister, Petronell. The boys played golf like their father, and went shooting and fishing; there was croquet and tennis as well. As Henry grew older, he loved to help on the estate – with threshing or getting in the corn – and if a new outhouse or granary was to be built, he would work away with the men. He had a special gift for music, too, and played the organ for church services whenever he was at home.

In fact, though, he was not often at home, for from the time when he stopped having a governess he had crossed the Irish Channel each term to go to boarding-school in England. Having to leave home so early made him self-sufficient and rather detached. At school he never seemed very enthusiastic about anything, but always worked hard and did his best. He found himself on the science side, and decided to try for a place at Cambridge. When he went up there for the entrance exam he was not inspired by the beauties of the place:

'Rather a boring day walking about trying to find something to see.'

He duly arrived at Trinity College, Cambridge, a shy bespectacled young man, in January 1919 – one of the younger undergraduates who were pouring up to Cambridge to fill up the war-depleted colleges alongside the older men who had survived the war. One of these older men at once took Henry under his wing, and three weeks after his arrival, his diary records, 'Discovered Norman Grubb was in Trinity, a cousin of mine and serious minded. Had tea with him.' This was the beginning of a great change in Henry's life. At last he was to find something which – in modern parlance – 'really turned him on'.

He worked hard at his chosen subject, mechanical sciences; he went skating on the frozen water-meadows most afternoons and enjoyed the D'Oyly Carte performances of Gilbert and Sullivan in the evenings; but more and more he found himself drawn to Norman Grubb's circle of friends – the 'serious minded' members of the CICCU (Cambridge Inter-Collegiate Christian Union). With them the chapel-religion of his schooldays and the faithful churchiness of his family seemed to come alive. Here were people who believed it, as he did, but who seemed inspired and fired by it. Life was fun with them, they had found some good news and seemed determined to share it.

Henry threw in his lot with them, and it may be that they were wise enough not to press him for an inner change before he was ready for it. At any rate he was never lonely now: they crowded in to tea in his rooms, ragging each other and scattering crumbs all over the floor; he went to Bible studies and prayer-meetings with them; sometimes they had serious talks.

One day Norman suggested something novel: someone was going to come and speak about beach-missions. Help was always needed with these children's missions round the coast in the summer vacation. They were great fun – why didn't Henry come along and find out more? And so in August, in a cheerful group of fifteen young people from

Cambridge, and under the leadership of an energetic clergyman called Mr Ovens, he went to Swanage. How enjoyable it all was – and hard work. There were games, competitions and picnics with the holidaying children, and time for bathing and tennis with his friends. The chief event of every day was the beach service – something quite new to Henry, when large crowds would gather round an elaborately made sandmodel – a Bible, a clock, a star – as pulpit, complete with Bible text. They would sing hymns and choruses in the sunshine (Henry played the harmonium and felt useful at once), and listen to the good news of the Gospel in words as fresh as the sea-breeze which ruffled their hair, while in the background the waves could be heard, breaking gently on the beach. It was during one of these meetings that Henry himself made what he called the 'essential transaction' with Jesus Christ, coming to him for cleansing and new life, and committing the rest of his life to him.

Back at home he tried to teach the household some choruses, but found it 'rather difficult to start from scratch'. Tragically, he had been home less than a month when it was discovered that little Petronell, who had been feverish for some days, had typhoid. She struggled against the illness for another week, but on October 3rd, aged 11 years and two months, she died. Henry grieved with the rest of the family as three days later the coffin went on the hay-float to the church. Then, back in Cambridge, sadly conscious now of how close even young people can be to death, he flung himself wholeheartedly into working for Christ.

Like all new converts, he was a bit too enthusiastic at first. Shy though he was, he collared all his old school-friends, determined to share the Gospel with them over tea. Some responded, others 'shied off religion quick'. Gradually he learnt a gentler approach, but his enthusiasm remained.

In December he went up to London for the first Inter-Varsity Conference, where among others his uncle George Grubb, a clergyman, was a speaker. It was at a missionary meeting here on December 9th that Henry first felt that 'I must go abroad somewhere, probably South America. The Lord will guide me.'

At home over Christmas, Henry began reading his namesake Barbrooke Grubb's books 'showing how he taught the Indians what religion was'. Henry may not have had Barbrooke Grubb's compelling personality, but he did have his capacity for endurance and hard work. The next two years show him taking more and more responsibility, working faithfully and enthusiastically for his Lord. He worked faithfully at his engineering studies, too, but they seemed to inspire him less and less. The mission to the university in February, his class at the Jesus Lane Sunday school, the open-air services on Parker's Piece and the possibility that God was calling him to work in the Argentine Chaco – these were the things that interested him. He was also planning, with the support of the local clergy, a mission to the churches in his part of Ireland.

At the end of February he went to visit Barbrooke Grubb at his home near Edinburgh, and his Easter vacation was taken up, with the help of Norman's brother, Kenneth Grubb, and one or two others, with the Irish mission. In fact things were not at all easy in Ireland at this time. The country had been on the brink of civil war when the Great War broke out, the revolutionary Fenianists wanting Home Rule and the Ulster Unionists opposing it.

As far back as April 25th, 1916, Henry had noted in his diary a Sinn Fein riot in Dublin, and the 'Troubles' had by no means resolved themselves since then. In 1920 Sinn Feiners were hunger-striking in Mountjoy prison, all shops were closed in sympathy and there was a general transport strike. In the same year the Government of Ireland Act split the country in two. For the Grubb family, part of the Protestant minority in the South, things were gradually growing more uncomfortable. Here, as elsewhere since the war, the seemingly unchangeable structure of society was beginning to crumble.

If Easter was busy, the summer vacation, too, was packed: a trip to Switzerland with his mother, then a visit to the

Keswick Convention. To Henry it seemed that 'so far only one message has been given to me: surrender all to Christ. ALL to thee is yielded.' At the missionary meeting he stood up 'to show that I was definitely dedicated to service in the foreign field'. The rest of the summer was spent helping with beach-missions. He loved 'the constant on-the-go which keeps one happy and satisfied'.

Soon he was on the go again in Cambridge; more so than ever as the war veterans had mostly gone down after their shortened courses and the people who had missed the war, now beginning their third year, found themselves in positions of leadership. It wasn't easy for them; they didn't have the glamour of the war heroes. Henry battled on, striving to win his friends for Christ, but often not quite persuading them. He longed to be more useful to God, and noted in his diary, 'Tea solo for a marvel, the first for a very long time. I wonder whether it is a mistake to see too many people and to become dependent on company for happiness and joy? It is a most undoubted failing.' An interesting remark in the light of future events.

On January 1st he wrote, 'Another year, in all probability the crux of my life. This year will see me finished at Cambridge and quite probably started on my life's work. As yet I don't even know what it is to be, but he who knows will direct and prepare me for it. Wherever he sends, let me be ready to go.'

It was a crucial year. Already Henry felt oppressed by a sense of the familiar order of things breaking up. His father's accounts were showing a deficit; his mother was unwell; his brother was going to South Africa. 'These last few nights are the last we shall all be together for the present. "Lovest thou me more than these?" Much harder than we imagine.' Being the eldest son, Henry must have wondered whether his father wanted him to settle on the estate and eventually take it over, but this potential conflict was resolved for him. The revolutionary violence in the south was growing worse, and the resulting feeling of insecurity preyed on his mother's health and nerves. His father realised that they must leave Ireland,

and so both parents were delighted that Henry seemed to have a plan for his life. They raised no objections to his plan that he go out to South America with SAMS, and Henry rejoiced, 'It is so good of God to have brought us all to be of one mind in our house about South America.'

Ardmayle was sold and a house bought in Bournemouth. When the local clergyman, Canon Pike, saw them off, he told them there had been a plan to kidnap Mr Grubb at the auction. They had got away just in time. In July 1921, SAMS accepted Henry for work in the Chaco, and after a short course in medical work for missionaries at Livingstone College in East London, he resolutely turned his back on England and his beloved Ireland, and set sail for South America.

6
Beginnings at Algarrobal

He arrived at Mision Chaqueña in 1922 to find a growing Christian colony in the care of only three men. Barbrooke Grubb, having established the mission in 1914, had since then been in uncertain health, had spent time both in Britain and in Paraguay, and had finally left South America for good in 1921. Other helpers had come and gone, and for a while only Richard Hunt and Edward Bernau, the two founder members who had come from Paraguay, were left. It is hard to find out much about these two men. As with some of the greatest of God's servants, they seemed to think nothing of themselves, and so remain shadowy figures, their achievements for God their only memorial.

Dr Bernau, as a younger missionary put it, 'was one of God's saints. I only saw him angry once. He was British, but I think his ancestors were Huguenots from France. He was medically trained, but not fully qualified – he had to stop his studies when his father died. He was a wonderful doctor.' Tall, with a long serious face, Edward Bernau had gone out to Paraguay in 1898, 'longing to be used for my Master's glory'. He had come to Argentina with Barbrooke Grubb in 1911, and was to work at Algarrobal (Mision Chaqueña) as the much loved doctor there until 1930. A gifted man of many interests, he was also an excellent carpenter and cabinet-maker, a repairer of watches and clocks, and an amateur astronomer. He had a telescope with which he used to study the stars over Algarrobal.

Richard Hunt had gone to Paraguay even earlier than Bernau – in 1894, after only elementary village schooling in England. For most of his working life, apart from extended leave every five years or so, he had to live separated from his wife, who was susceptible to malaria and allergic to quinine and so had to live in England. He, too, came first to the cane-fields and then to Algarrobal with Barbrooke Grubb, and finally left in 1929.

Bishop Every described him as 'not only our language genius, but the father and mother of this Mataco mission'. Indeed, he took a fatherly interest in everyone on the mission, and loved to talk to them. Each evening at sunset as the women fetched water from the pump and everyone went about his business after the evening service, he would wander out in the compound, ready to chat and to listen to everyone he met. Bishop Every also observed that, 'A first-rate capable lay-missionary, he was ordained late in life. His watchword was patient, solid teaching based on a knowledge of the Mataco mentality and character, which grew with his ever-increasing knowledge of the language.' And this knowledge was unique. He was recognised as an authority on Indian languages by the University of Tucuman.

The third missionary was a much younger man, Alfred Tompkins, who had been at Algarrobal for less than a year. His father, at one time a cooper who made barrels for the margarine made from the fat of slaughtered animals in London's cattle market, went out to Argentina in 1914 to work in the cattle trade there, and in 1915 the rest of the family joined him. 'We were a Christian family. I remember a butcher friend seeing my father go by on his way to church while we were still in England and saying, "I guess that's the only man in the cattle market who goes to church!"' The family settled happily in Buenos Aires, took lessons in Spanish, and joined in with the Anglican chaplaincy church.

One winter day in 1921, Alfred was invited to see the bishop in Buenos Aires, Bishop Every. Bishop Every had succeeded Bishop Stirling on his retirement in 1900, and was now based in Buenos Aires, where St John's church had become the pro-cathedral of the new Anglican Bishopric in Argentina in 1910.

It was a very cold night and I went to see him in his 'palace' at the back of the cathedral. It consisted of one bedroom, one big study/living room and a bathroom. The bishop was English, and a bachelor. There were a lot of English people in Argentina at that time, working on the railways, on ranches, in the banks and in the import and export business, following the Treaty of Commerce and friendship between the two countries of 1825; and he was their bishop. I sat beside his blazing fire and wondered why he was starting to tell me all the history and geography of the Chaco missions. Eventually he came to the point: 'There are only two men at Algarrobal now: Richard Hunt and Edward Bernau. Bernau hasn't had leave since before the war. He must get away. We want somebody to go and keep Hunt company until he gets back, and you are the man!'

Tompkins went for six months and stayed for twenty-four years.

So he was there – young, cheerful, confident, fresh from Buenos Aires – when Henry Grubb arrived. Tompkins recalled the meeting: 'He appeared to be a very shy young man. I still remember his brief reply when introduced – just two words: "Hello Tompkins", and that without lifting his eyes!' In fact Henry rarely met anyone's eyes, a peculiarity which people found hard to understand. It was on account of an eye condition caused by too much reading during a childhood attack of measles. He was the first missionary to come to the area wearing steel-rimmed spectacles, and was soon named *Techinas* – 'iron-eyes' – by the Indians. Quickly Tompkins discovered that he had a sense of humour, and they were soon enjoying learning Mataco together. There were so many strange words to learn, and so many of them seemed to be the names of exotic Chaco birds, that whenever a new word came up which stumped Henry, he would have Tompkins in stitches by wryly speculating, 'a bird?'

Four Englishmen in a little Christian community on the edge of the Chaco; what was the situation in which they found themselves? When the pioneers had arrived in 1914, there had only been two rough squatters' huts beside a stagnant pool among the algarrobo trees which gave the place its name. The estate was about half a mile wide, stretching from the rough road which took supplies south-eastwards into the Chaco from Embarcacion, as far as the River Bermejo which ran parallel with the road. At this time, no Indians lived on the estate. The Argentine Chaco – the flat area of land between the Rivers Bermejo and Pilco-mayo to the south and north, with the Andes to the west and the River Paraguay to the east – was already undergoing change. The railway, recently extended northwards from Tucuman to Embarcacion, was making the area more accessible and bringing settlers flooding in.

The coming of the settlers brought a dramatic diminution in the Indian population, as they succumbed, untended, to European diseases or were slaughtered in punitive military expeditions.[9] On the other hand, as we have seen, in the beautiful hillier parts of the country to the south-west, the sugar-cane plantations were providing seasonal work for thousands of Indians. It was at this crucial time of change for the Indian population that God brought the 'white people from over the sea' to come and help them. Significantly, they called these white visitors *wajchas*, 'tail of the water', whereas their name for the Spanish-speaking whites was *ahattai* – devils.

Once some basic buildings had been erected at Algar-robal, a few local Indians began to show an interest in what was going on, in particular an elderly man named Joaquin who lived with his wife and children near by and who spent most of his time fishing and gardening or cutting firewood for a squatter. With the ruthlessness sometimes shown by men of vision, Barbrooke Grubb had gently but firmly moved this old man and his family on to the estate. When he showed reluctance, his belongings were simply picked up and moved for him. 'In that way,' as Richard Hunt comments, 'the first settler was secured, and he never regretted the removal. Still stubborn, a confirmed grumbler, something of a recluse, he continued for many years staunch to the mission and faithful in his work as water-man.'[10] The ice broken, others wanted to follow suit. As Hunt put it, 'They had been harassed by white settlers, often ill-treated and despised, cheated and browbeaten. The idea of a friendly foreigner and a safe refuge appealed to them, and in the course of a few months some six families came and settled there; each with a house and garden, and with freedom to come and go as they liked.'

Soon an open-air school was started where the children learnt to read and write in their own language and in Spanish, and to count and measure, as well as a little of the geography of Argentina; games, including football which soon became popular, and some simple hymns and Bible stories. A rough building was erected which served for teaching and for worship. A cattle farm was also established, which provided training for the Indians in numerous skills. The mission was observed and admired by other Indians passing on their way to the sugar-cane estates, and news of it spread.

In 1919 all the mission buildings and property had to be moved to a temporary site farther from the river because of disastrous flooding of the River Bermejo, but eventually, in spite of all the difficulties, a Mataco of unusual intelligence and character called Martin Ibarra became the first convert, and in 1922 shortly before Henry Grubb arrived, nine Matacos were baptised by Bishop Every.

I met Guilfredo Ibarra, Martin's son, an ordained pastor and now an elderly man, at Algarrobal in 1987. He described his father as 'a very strong man who had killed people. Arrows and bullets wouldn't go into him! He was the elected leader – the *cacique* or local chief. He and his family had settled in this area about six years before the missionaries came, and later moved on to the mission itself.' Guilfredo remembered Barbrooke Grubb coming in 1914 – a big strong man who loved the people – and taking him, a small child then, in his arms. As he put it, evil spirits had instilled into people's minds the idea that people would come who would eat them. 'It was my father, the Capitan, who placated them and settled their minds about accepting the missionaries. He said, "I'll go and see them. If they eat me, I don't care. If they don't, then you can follow me."'

Guilfredo also remembered Richard Hunt, 'a lovable man. Very loving with the Indians. He smoked a pipe. He would go along to the witch-doctor and listen to him. He learnt our language and wrote it down. He had a walking-stick which came to have thirty-seven notches – one for every rattlesnake he had killed.

'Henry Grubb rode a white mule and wore imported breeches and boots; Alfred Tompkins we called "Stiff Elbow", because in the store he only just let the scales go down when he was weighing out the goods. Dr Bernau took photographs. He had a telescope and let me look through it to see the moon. When we saw all this, we said we wanted the missionaries to stay here. Chiefs travelling through Algarrobal on their way to the cane-fields would ask my father, "What are these people doing here?" He'd say, "They are doing a lot of good." Eventually they handed over a lot of their charms to Richard Hunt. They thought he would die, but he told them, "If you hand them in to me and I don't die, that will show you how strong my God is."

'Eventually in 1922,' Guilfredo went on, 'the first Christians, including my mother and father, were baptised.'

When asked why there was such a long time – eight years – from the coming of the missionaries to the first baptism, Guilfredo explained that it was because the missionaries didn't lay down the law to the people. They allowed the Holy Spirit to work gradually, teaching them about drunkenness and so on, and this took time. This explanation is interesting in view of the comment often made that the missionaries suppressed Indian customs – in particular the drinking feasts and the dancing that went with them.

The first reference to this question occurs in the Algarrobal mission journal for 1916, which records in December 'a conference with Joaquin, Ernesto, Mateo and Joaquincito over the drink question. Decided to put a stop to it' – the interesting thing here being that missionaries and Indians conferred and reached the decision together. Sadly, 'the drink question' recurred from time to time, and although Richard Hunt rejoiced in a SAMS annual report that 'Martin, our first convert, who had been used to the drink till he was over 40, abstained from it for three years before his baptism', the journal for December 1922 records 'suspicions that beer has been made and consumed in very small quantities. Martin admitted that he had tasted it. I spoke to him and the other culprits very solemnly. I believe they were truly repentant.'

So there they were: two experienced missionaries, two younger men, and by now about 150 Indians, still often morose, ungrateful and prone to grumble, but gradually growing in confidence, a few now committed to Christ, living in temporary buildings on a site which could well be devastated by flooding yet again. How would things develop from there? Was this small beginning doomed to failure, or was it the start of something significant for the people of 'the land between the rivers'?

7
Looking North

More helpers gradually joined the team: Alfred Tompkins married, his wife Gertrude becoming the first woman missionary to work among the Matacos; and a young medical student from Edinburgh, Colin Smith, was sent out by Barbrooke Grubb to help Dr Bernau. He came out with a friend of his, an art student called John Arnott. William Everitt arrived at Algarrobal, too, in 1925 – a tall, strong young man who had recently sold up his building firm in Suffolk and given most of the proceeds to SAMS before coming out himself. Until now, Edward Bernau had done much of the building work at Algarrobal, as the Matacos had continued to trust their witch-doctors rather than his

The church at Algarrobal.

medical skills. He had designed and built the first Anglican
church in the Argentine Chaco, and there it stood, completed
in 1926, the church of St Michael and All Angels, the focus of
the mission 'compound' at Algarrobal. Sturdy, simple and
dignified, with its strong wooden pillars supporting the roof,
the building had used 160 algarrobo trunks, each so long that
six Indians were needed to carry it.

Now, as the Indians began to turn to the mission for
medical help, William Everitt took responsibility for the
buildings. He enlarged and strengthened the church, a task
that was completed in 1930. As Guilfredo Ibarra put it,
'William Everitt renewed all things and strengthened them,
and so they remain to this day.' Simple strong furniture was
made, too, for the church to William's designs, and the
carpentering techniques which he taught the Indians then
formed the basis of the furniture industry which became an
enduring feature of the mission's work.

Then in 1925 the mission faced a crisis, when one of the
Indians living on the mission went berserk in the middle of
the night and murdered his wife and mother-in-law. The
traditional Mataco reaction to a terrible event of this sort was
the vendetta, and anxiety and edginess were immediately
evident throughout the mission as the relatives of the dead
women prepared to take their revenge. An eruption of violence seemed imminent, and probably the break-up of the
mission, when on Christmas morning Martin Ibarra, speaking with remarkable spiritual power, persuaded his own
people to follow Christ's way – the way of peace. This was a
turning-point, and from then onwards the Christian community at Algarrobal began to grow and to mature. Its work
was not to end here, either: indeed, this was only the
beginning, and the next move, already planned some years
earlier by Barbrooke Grubb, was to be northwards into
Bolivia.

The idea of a mission in Bolivia was not new. The Franciscans had worked there in the previous two centuries, as
described earlier, and it was to Bolivia that Allen Gardiner
had come in 1846. Protestants of the Eastern Bolivian

Mission had been working there, too, for some years and, in addition, in 1923 Barbrooke Grubb and the South American Missionary Society had received an official request from the Bolivian Government to start work, aided by them, in their country.

It is important to distinguish motives here. The motive of the missionaries was simple: the good, both spiritual and temporal, of the Chaco Indians. To this end, also in 1923, Barbrooke Grubb had succeeded in drawing up a legal trust aimed at securing the social and religious rights of the Indians in the connection with the Chaco Indian Co-operative Society, based in Paraguay. In particular certain land rights had been obtained for them there. As he wrote in a letter to his sister-in-law at this time: 'The Chaco Trust Deed has been completed and signed. The future of the Chaco is now placed on a solid basis, and the faith to be taught secured on the good old lines. The future now depends upon succeeding new men having the grit and courage to put it through.[11]

Realistically, he went on in the same letter: 'Difficulties, however, are ahead. We have succeeded only too well. The Chaco is opening up fast.' In fact various business interests, including oil prospectors, had their eyes on the Chaco, and Bolivian officials had observed how already in certain areas the work of the missionaries had made the country safe for occupation. As Richard Hunt comments in his biography of Grubb, 'They not only recognised the value of missionary work, but urged the missionaries to undertake similar work in their own territory, so that the wild tribes might be brought under control and the district colonised.'

We see here how the philanthropic and spiritual aims of the missionaries and the temporal and mercenary aims of governments and businesses became intertwined, and Barbrooke Grubb was well aware of the need for wise leaders to take over from him in the Chaco mission, if the total good – mental, spiritual and physical – of the Indians was to result. Certainly he had promising material in his namesake, Henry Grubb, and it was Henry who was chosen to lead the first exploratory trip northwards from the Argentine Chaco into Bolivia in 1925.

Having made careful preparations, which included in Henry's case a three months' course in Spanish at Cordoba, they set off on June 24th – four of them: Henry on a white mule; William Everitt; Ramon, a Chiriguano guide, much needed as most of the time they would be travelling through Chiriguano country, and Antonio, a young Mataco Christian. Ramon proved valuable as an interpreter, but hopeless as a guide. 'At one thing, however, he excelled,' recalled Henry, 'and that was at eating.' They made him the cook.

' "Now we're off," we shouted – but we weren't, for before we had gone a hundred yards, the pack on the pack-mule bearing our luggage had shifted and we had to readjust it. Again we started amid cheers, and a few moments later we were once more adjusting the pack.' Eventually they were really on their way, and the first night was spent at Embarcacion. Starting at dawn each day and sleeping at night on their saddlery on the ground, they reached Tartagal two days later, a small 'camp' town which by now the railway had reached. As Henry commented on the people he saw here:

> One has only to see the Indians who live in these places to realise what our so-called civilisation does for them. The men, half-starved and dirty, roam the streets and pick up a few cents at odd jobs, the women sell their bodies for a few cents to make a living. All are wracked by disease, and either die, uncared for and alone, or linger on, a miserable hopeless community. We saw some Matacos here, but what a difference to those on the mission with their cheerful laughter, bright faces and happy lives. Would that those who cry down missionary work could see the change the Gospel makes, not only in the life, but in the appearance.

This was why Henry, as Barbrooke Grubb before him, was eager to reach 'the great Indian hiding-place' – the Chaco – before other settlers. As he commented, 'Experience has shown us that when the missionary is first upon the scene, the native is better prepared to withstand the devastating effects of modern civilising forces.'

The pioneering party followed the route that Barbrooke Grubb had taken in his exploratory trip of 1910. Soon the frontier was crossed at Yacuiba, a pleasant town of neat white-washed houses and orange trees. The next night they received hospitality at the old Franciscan mission of Aguairenda, and after three more days' travelling they reached a large Mataco village on the banks of the River Pilcomayo. This was the point at which Allen Gardiner had so impressed the Indians by swimming across the river. Its real banks here, Henry noted, were about a kilometre apart, although it was far from full at this time. To the west could be seen the mountains where the river had its source. The party camped for a few days, and soon attracted crowds of Matacos who seemed eager for the missionaries to come and settle with them, and gave them much useful information.

They then waded across the river and found themselves among the Chiriguanos who inhabited the northern bank. These were the people among whom the Jesuits and Franciscans mostly worked, and the small town of Villa Montes here was the place where the Franciscans had struggled for twenty years to run their mission, San Francisco. Farther on, the little group came to Tarairi, one of the larger Franciscan settlements. Here, as elsewhere, the work of the mission seemed to be on the decline.

Riding on through pleasantly hilly country, they eventually reached the village of San Antonio on the River Parapiti, where they were welcomed by John Linton, a Methodist of the Eastern Bolivian Mission, who had been there for ten years.

In case the reader is confused, let me explain that two places called San Antonio feature in this story, and they were quite near to each other. On the one hand, San Antonio was the name given by the Franciscans to one of their two missions on opposite banks of the Pilcomayo where Villa Montes now is; but San Antonio del Parapiti is considerably

farther north on the River Parapiti, and here John Linton
had a Protestant mission.

The visitors were impressed by the lovely garden John
Linton had made on the previously bare hillside where the
mission stood overlooking the wide River Parapiti, newly
emerged from its narrow gorge through the mountains on to
the flat plains below.

During the evening, as Henry recorded in his diary, 'Mr
Linton explained his mission and his conflicts with priests
and politicians. He holds the position of national school-
teacher and has all the government on his side. The priests
have no power to move him for that reason.' Interestingly, he
also notes on visiting the school the next day, that 'all
teaching takes place in Spanish, Guarani being forbidden in
the school.' The party spent several days with John Linton,
learning many interesting things about the local Indians,
then pushed on northwards to Charagua. It seemed, from
what John Linton said, that the white people in this part of
Bolivia, being very much in the minority, treated the Indians
very harshly, using them in effect as slaves.

'It is amazing to reflect,' comments Henry, 'that many of
our fellow creatures are still to this day [1925] given no legal
status . . . to kill an Indian is not, therefore, murder, any
more than killing a wild deer in the forest.' At about this time,
however, the Bolivian Government did grant the
Chiriguanos full rights of citizenship.

At Charagua, for the first time, they seem to have departed
from the route followed by Barbrooke Grubb fifteen years
earlier, and travelled eastwards through the district of Izozo.
The country was wild, and one day they saw 'deer, hare,
puma, ostrich, the tracks of the ant-eater and heard a jaguar
barking'. Reaching the banks of the Parapiti again, they met
some Guarani-speaking Chiriguano Indians who seemed
very anxious for a mission, and then leaving the river
travelled through thick *monte*, or woodland, infested with
ticks, and then through equally wild desert country covered
with low wiry cactus known as *chagua*. Eventually they
crossed the Rio Grande and reached Santa Cruz just in time

to witness the centenary celebrations of Bolivia's independence. From there they travelled southwards again, following a slightly different route, and arrived back at Algarrobal in September. They had been away just three months and covered about a thousand miles.

8

Adventures in Bolivia

The Bolivian mission of SAMS has a place in this story as being the first missionary outreach from Algarrobal. Following the exploratory trip of the previous year, it was decided to set up a mission among the Chiriguanos, the Guarani-speaking Indians of Izozo whom Allen Gardiner had visited eighty years before. He had been refused permission to live with them, but now they seemed keen for a mission.

In July 1926, therefore, four people set off from Algarrobal to respond to this call: Henry Grubb, William Everitt and John Arnott on muleback, and Salomon, an Argentine boy, who drove the luggage cart. The hillier country of Bolivia caused them problems with the cart. According to Henry, 'The long descents meant that gradually the speed increased, first to a trot, then to a gallop, and then to a flying stampede with the mules doing their best to keep ahead of the cart.' With Salomon screeching and whoopeeing with delight, they hurtled to the bottom. Mercifully no harm was done, but the prudent and practical Everitt soon fixed up a brake. It took them six weeks to cover four hundred miles, and the trip seemed as though it would never come to an end. It did, though, and the Izozo Indians were surprised and delighted to see them again.

The chief, Enrique Yambae, lent them a mud and wattle house with a thatched roof and no windows, in the small village of Aguaraigua where he himself lived. They stayed there for six months while building their own house. Apart from the hot north wind, which when it blew brought clouds of sand from the nearby river-bed, they were comfortable enough. But the sand got into everything – their eyes, their mouths, their ears, their beds, their papers, their food. When food came on the table, they promptly had to cover their plates with another plate, and then scoop out their food from between.

In the evenings, when the Indians had finished working in their gardens, the missionaries gathered them together for a service. Yambae, who knew a little Spanish as well as Guarani, acted as interpreter, but as Henry commented, 'At first we were delighted with how well things seemed to be going, but as our knowledge of Guarani increased, we re-alised that Yambae's ideas of interpretation were very different from ours and that a lot of his views on all sorts of subjects were getting thrown in with our talks. Preaching by interpretation on the mission field is full of snares and we soon decided it was preferable to do without.' In fact, Yambae soon met with tragedy, as Henry records.

'One evening, after the service was over, Mr Arnott and I were sitting chatting when a figure appeared in the dark doorway, which was hardly ever closed. He came forward into the light and we saw that it was Yambae, with a black eye, and somewhat the worse for drink. "I've killed my wife," said he.

'"You've what?" we exclaimed, as he and his wife had always seemed an affectionate couple.

'"We were drinking," he said, "and then we quarrelled. She started to hit me with a piece of wood and I struck her with my fist behind the ear. She fell and the people say she is dead."

'Leaving my companion to talk to the rapidly sobering Yambae, I went down to the village, about a hundred yards distant, and found a silent group gathered round the body of the woman, whom they were even then laying out for burial. She was dead all right, and the story of the bystanders corresponded with what Yambae had told us: it was a case of manslaughter.

'I was puzzled what to do. Obviously the authorities should be informed, but the only local authority was a sort of non-official policeman who lived on the outskirts of the village. I went to see him, late as it then was. He did not know what he ought to do, but thought he should arrest Yambae

pending investigations. We walked up to the mission house,
only to find Mr Arnott alone.

'"Where's Yambae?" we asked.

'"Oh, he went away. I had no authority to detain him," he
said. It turned out that he had set out there and then to walk
to Argentina, where he had many relations, and where the
arm of Bolivian law could not reach him. Perhaps it was the
easiest way out for all of us. He later told us that he felt it was
God's punishment to him for refusing to accept the Gospel.
We kept in touch with Yambae for several years; he became
an earnest Christian and a preacher of the Gospel among his
own people in Argentina, but he never returned to Izozo.'

Henry comments here on the curse that drink was among
the Izozo Indians. Home brewed from maize, gallons of
'*chicha*' were consumed, especially at Carnival time – the
three days of licence before Lent. 'The waste of maize, which
has a high nutritional value, on these feasts was tragic. We
preached against them from the start of the work, but
Carnival was a time of temptation which few of the early
converts were able to resist.'

A year or two passed and the work was developing nicely.
Some of the Chiriguanos were becoming interested in the
Gospel, when something happened which could have put a
sudden end to it all.

Rumours began to reach us that some people were trying
to get Protestant missionaries removed from the country.
The Bolivian-Paraguayan war was then working up, spy
fever was prevalent, so it had only to be whispered that we
were spies to set the authorities after us. But who was it
who wanted to get us out and why? Not the local people.
Suffice it to say that, as we found out later, the pocket of a
certain gentleman had been touched when Mr Linton had
been forced to reveal some shady dealings in which the
man was engaged, since they would have meant defraud-
ing the Indians of many thousands of Bolivianos (the
Bolivian currency). But that gentleman had friends in the
government to whom he hinted that Protestant mission-

aries (including Mr Linton) were in reality spies of Paraguay. The fact that SAMS had a mission in Paraguay was well known, which seemed to prove that the insinuation was true, and so an order was given that Mr Linton and the leader of the Izozo mission (myself) were to be arrested forthwith and deported from the country.

One day I received a message asking me to call on a neighbour who lived some four miles away. Although I suspected that something more than a friendly call was in the air, I rode over and found an officer and a squad of soldiers in the house. 'You are now our prisoner, and may not return to Aguaraigua,' they told me. In due course we set out for Charagua, where we stayed at the barracks for a few days, and then, after picking up Mr Linton at San Antonio, headed for the frontier. When we were passing through a town, we had to ride in pairs, a prisoner with a soldier alongside, but the rest of the time we rode as we liked. Each soldier carried his rifle fully loaded and placed across his saddle so that he sat on it. I used to take care to keep at the butt end of the rifles in case one went off, but fortunately none did.

There was a small garrison at Villa Montes, so there we had to look like prisoners again, and were put to sleep in a room guarded by a sentry. Next day we went on. The Pilcomayo was in full flood, and Mataco Indians were commandeered to swim the animals across, one in front with the halter in his hand and the other holding the tail and giving encouragement with a switch from behind. We crossed by boat. Hardly had we mounted again than the rain began to fall in earnest – it was the height of the wet season. We took shelter in the disused mission buildings of the old Franciscan mission on the south bank of the river. We stayed there for twenty-four hours. There was not a stick of furniture in the place, but at least we were dry. Eventually we got back to Algarrobal.

In fact, after some months of diplomacy, the expulsion order was withdrawn and both Henry and John Linton returned to Bolivia. In the meantime a new missionary, Leslie Harwood, went out to Izozo, and a little later the Rev. Ernest Panter, of whom more later. The work prospered; a school was started; and in 1930 the first converts, Manuel and Nicolas, were baptised at Aguaraigua. Shortly after that the mission was visited by Bishop Every – or almost wasn't, as mules, cart, missionaries, bishop and all were nearly lost in the quicksands of the Parapiti.

Gradually Henry Grubb spent more time at Algarrobal, especially with the retirement in 1929 of the superintendent, Richard Hunt. Not only had Henry set up the Bolivian work of SAMS, he had also translated John's Gospel into Guarani and made a dictionary as well. When he left, Ernest Panter took over the leadership at Izozo. Another man, fresh from England, who joined the team in 1930 was Alfred Tebboth, and he remembers the mission at this time.

We were always evangelising in the villages on both sides of the Parapiti – especially Ernest Panter. He was a really dedicated Christian. He had his funny ideas: for instance meals always took a long time as he chewed everything thirty times. We had a house with a room for each of us, and a school which was also used as the church. Harwood did the medical work, I did the school and Panter concentrated on the spiritual side.

In Bolivia the Indians and the white people were friendly, unlike in Argentina. We held services in Spanish for the settlers. The forebears of these Indians had been involved in the Jesuit and Franciscan missions, so these people had learnt to work together. The Indians used to wear a stud of wood and metal in their lower lip, and their faces were painted. It has to be said that we didn't make many converts, but a few did become strong Christians.

Once, years later, I was travelling through Los Blancos in Argentina and people were telling me about a wonderful Indian, Manuel, who was pastoring a group of believers. It was the same Manuel who had been one of our first converts at Izozo.

But then came the Paraguayan-Bolivian war, and in 1935 the advancing Paraguayans swept over Izozo, so that all the inhabitants including the missionaries had to evacuate northwards to Santa Cruz. From there the missionaries made their way, some to England and some to Algarrobal, to rejoin the work in Argentina. The Guarani-speaking Indians were taken by soldiers to Paraguay, where a similar language was spoken, and they settled down there.

When the war ended it was decided not to reopen the Izozo mission, which was very isolated, but Leslie Harwood stayed in Bolivia as an independent worker, later married a Bolivian Christian called Modesta and carried on the work with her help. The work still goes on. Modesta, who speaks both Spanish and Guarani, continued Leslie's translation work after his sudden death, and their daughter Januit and her husband share in the work, too, in Santa Cruz.

The work of SAMS in Bolivia lasted for less than ten years, but it was taken up by others, and was part of the pattern God was weaving for the Chaco. Like the Indian women themselves, carefully selecting wool and spinning it into thread, dyeing it and weaving it into complex patterns, so God was carefully choosing his people – selecting them to reach out to the despised Chaco Indians with his love.

Several years earlier, in the small English coastal village of East Runton, another thread needed for God's weaving in the Chaco was being prepared, or spun.

Spinning wool.

9
A Fisherman's Son

'And please God, don't let me die tonight.'

Alfred Leake, the 8-year-old son of a local fisherman, lay in Cromer hospital seriously ill with tubercular peritonitis. Tossing and feverish and in considerable pain, he thought back to his home – Pond Cottage – at East Runton, where every night he had been used to kneel at his mother's knee in front of the glowing fire; and to the prayer she had taught him there, he added this prayer of his own. God graciously answered, and although he left hospital rather worse than he went in, his mother's care and plenty of fresh air and sunshine gradually did their work and he grew well and strong again.

For Alfred, his brothers Clem and David and sister Olive, East Runton was a wonderful place to grow up in. Donkeys and ponies grazed on the commons. The milkman would come each morning and ladle fresh milk into a jug at the door, and various bakers would make their daily rounds with lovely crusty bread often still hot from the oven. The fishermen, Alfred's father among them, would clatter down the street and on to the beach in their heavy leather, hobnailed sea-boots and be off after their catch at any hour of the day or night according to the tides.

The children were rarely bored, for if they were not helping their parents, as they often were, there was always something to do: playing on the common, paddling or bathing on the beach, playing or helping in the fields. There were special occasions, too – the visits of the windmill man exchanging paper windmills for jamjars, the Italian hokey-pokey man with his half-penny cornets, the organ-grinder with his monkey, and the man with the dancing bear. And every Saturday the all-important visit to the sweet shop, to spend the weekly halfpenny on chameleon-coloured aniseed balls or black liquorice.

The Leake children had the benefit of a loving Christian home. Their father's father was a deep-sea fisherman and had been a heavy drinker. He was converted in Cromer Church, and impressed young Alfred by telling him that whereas in Grimsby they used to tie up and make for the nearest pub, after he was converted they'd make for the Salvation Army citadel! Their other grandfather, a sailor who had travelled the world and taken part in the gold-rush in Australia, was one of the founders of the Primitive Methodist church in Runton. The children attended the village Sunday school, and later on a Bible class run by the parish lady worker, who had been a missionary in China.

By 1911, when he was 10, Alfred was well enough to go back to the village school, after two years' absence, and he left at 14. By then, of course, it was wartime. The war meant a great deal of change, and much sadness for the village. When he left school in 1915, Alfred spent the summer at sea with his father, then got a job as a paper-boy. Visiting the different houses in the neighbourhood, he realised how much people had suffered and lost.

The war ended and men started coming back to Runton. A few were badly maimed, and many, having given up their livelihoods to go to the front, could find no work when they returned. Alfred by now was working in the local garage. He was happy enough, but gradually as time went on, he began to feel restless. Should he not be doing more with his life? God had preserved him from almost certain death when a child. And then, during the war, others had suffered so much and he had sacrificed nothing.

His sister, Olive, had by now given up her job because she believed that God was calling her to train as a nurse. Might not God have a similar job for him? By the time he was 19, Alfred was convinced that God was indeed calling him to something, but to what? A practical person, not studious, and very shy – what could he do? Finally one day Alfred came home as usual from the garage, had his tea and changed, and jumped on his bike to go and talk to Mr Fitch, the local vicar.

'Come in boy, come in. And what can I do for you?' Mr Fitch sat the gawky young garage-hand down by his fireside and listened while he stammered out his rather vague idea that God wanted him to serve him in some way. Poor Mr Fitch did his best, but he was baffled. The only thing he could think of was to talk to the Buxtons, the well-known Norfolk family who took a great interest in the social and spiritual welfare of the village and who had an estate somewhere in Africa, Mr Fitch thought.

He tied a knot in his handkerchief to remind himself about it, and sent Alfred home. Perhaps the knot came untied. Anyway, the months went by, but nothing happened. Nor did anything come of a few other ideas Alfred tried. Then, after about a year, the guidance he sought came in a most unexpected place: the reading-room in Runton. Drifting in one day in September 1923, Alfred idly picked up a news-paper – and there he saw a small advertisement from the Church Army, an organisation of which he had never even heard, saying that they wanted men who may have had only an elementary education, but who were willing to be trained for various departments of their work.

Alfred was astounded. A clear call at last! He applied, and was accepted for a short probationary course in London. Training was hard. After long days of chores and lectures, six evenings a week were spent at Speakers' Corner, Hyde Park, where the young trainees were supposed to take it in turns to address the crowd. Alfred's turn duly came, and he worked hard at preparing what he wanted to say. Up on the stand, he looked down at the crowd. Horrors! Everything he had planned to say went clean out of his head, and not a word would come. His colleagues kindly sang a chorus while he retreated in confusion. Surely this spelled the end of the Church Army for him! Alfred takes up the tale.

Two days to Black Friday, the day when we probationary recruits would learn our fate. A thoughtful mate came up:

'Well, you'll be going home again then, brother!'

'What, me? Why do you say that?'

'You can't *speak*, can you? They don't have anyone in the Church Army who can't speak!'

Encouraged by these cheering words, I sat with the others in the lecture room on the fateful day. Every name had been read out except mine – all either to go home as unsuitable or to stay on in one of the various departments. Last of all my name was read out. I was to go into the social welfare side, which meant helping in hostels and labour homes – places where poor men with no homes could go and live and work.

After further training with the Church Army, I was sent to Birkenhead on Merseyside, and was put in charge of the wood-yard, where men spent their time chopping and bundling kindling wood for a small wage. I shall always be grateful to God for those years on Merseyside. It was just the sort of experience I needed, and prepared me for the work which God had planned for me, thousands of miles away in the forests of South America. I learnt to take responsibility, gradually I even learnt to speak in public, but one of the greatest lessons I learnt was not to take a man's behaviour at its face value. If we could only know what these people had been through; what they are up against, and why they behave as they do – we would often treat them very differently.

It was during his time with the Church Army, too, that Alfred, who had heard the Christian message from childhood, came to a fuller understanding of what Christ had done for him on the Cross: 'From then onwards I was set free to serve him out of love and gratitude, rather than out of a sense of duty.'

He stayed with the Church Army for a few years, but still he felt that his life's work was to be something different, and farther afield. From childhood the idea of travel had absorbed and fascinated him; through his seafaring antecedents it was in his blood. Night after night as a boy he used to lie in bed reading *The Swiss Family Robinson*, *Martin Rattler* and similar books, by the light of his paraffin lamp. And the ex-missionary lady-worker had fired his imagination, too. He realised he probably couldn't be a missionary himself – he hadn't studied enough – but he thought he might be able to help in some sort of pioneer work on the practical side.

Funnily enough, his call came through a newspaper again. Glancing through the *Liverpool Echo* one evening, he saw a SAMS meeting advertised, and decided to go. As a result of what he heard, the enquiries he made, and a subsequent interview, it was arranged that he would go out to work with SAMS in Argentina.

'They gave me a wonderful send-off in Runton and then I set off from the Beach station in Cromer. I chose that way because it meant going over the bridge in East Runton and catching a last glimpse of my old home.' He sailed from Southampton in March 1927. Also going out were Dr Bernau, returning after his furlough, Yolande Royce – the first qualified nurse to go out to Algarrobal – and Ted Nye, who had previously been in Paraguay. For Alfred there were no regrets – only feelings of thankfulness, dedication and excitement: at last he was on his way to his life's work!

10

The Pilcomayo Seen at Last

We have watched how one and another 'thread' has been selected over the years by God for his weaving in the Argentine Chaco. Slowly he gathered the men and women of his choice to work for him there. But the most important people have remained invisible. Just as in the Chaco itself the Indian settlements are often hidden among the green forest trees, so the Indians (or Amerindians) in this story remain shadowy figures.

For centuries they had wandered over the plains and forests of central South America and, because of their inaccessibility and the poorness of their land, were not reached by the Spanish-speaking colonists as quickly as those nearer the coasts. More recently, settlers had begun to encroach upon their land, eager for ostrich-feathers and furs, introducing alcohol and guns, their goats and cattle grazing the earth bare. This led to feuds as well as food shortages, and together with the onslaught of white men's diseases, thousands of Indians died.

By 1927, these changes were markedly affecting even the Indians in their remote villages on the Pilcomayo. As Richard Hunt put it, 'A generation ago, the Mataco were calculated to be 100,000 strong, but it would be difficult to find 30,000 today among all the clans. During the last hundred and twenty years civilisation has gradually overspread this region. The novel conditions introduced with civilisation have almost shattered the fabric of social life.'

Let us go with Alfred Leake, as six months after his arrival he sets off on muleback with Colin Smith, the leader of the expedition, and Severo, a Mataco Christian from Algarrobal, to visit the Mataco villages along the Argentine bank of the river, to make sure that a mission among them would be welcomed.

The Pilcomayo! Bishop Every wrote that for him, from his first coming to South America, the Pilcomayo River had always held certain elements of the mysterious unknown. Many years back, on his first visits to the mission stations in Paraguay, Barbrooke Grubb had spoken to him of it, far away to the west beyond endless palm forests, 'so that when twenty-six years afterwards I arrived at our new mission station from the other side, almost my first act was to go down to the river as if making a religious pilgrimage – the Pilcomayo of my dreams seen at last!'[12]

The missionary party investigating the possibility of this new mission had set off from Algarrobal on September 5th, 1927. They had been invited, curiously enough, by a Texan cowboy, John Fitzgerald, who had come over several years earlier with Tex Rickard. Rickard had made a great deal of money by promoting a famous boxing match in 1910 when the American negro heavyweight, Jack Johnson, had defeated Jim Jeffries, 'the white man's hope'. With this money, although intending eventually to go to Paraguay, he had bought a concession of land on the Argentine bank of the Pilcomayo.

The colony was a failure, and by 1927 only Fitzgerald was left. A good friend of the Indians, and possibly feeling that they would be less trouble if rather more civilised, he approached Richard Hunt about the possibility of a mission among them, and even helped to negotiate a gift of a small piece of land adjoining the nearby Indian reserve. This became the site of the first mission settlement on the river, San Andres.

The mission party found Fitzgerald and his family living for the time being in a grass hut at a place called Media Luna. They stayed the night, and next day pushed on to the river, which they found to be about eighty yards wide at this point, smooth and quite fast flowing, too shallow to be navigable. Here they had their first glimpse of the local Indians: 'fine looking fellows, many carrying bows and arrows or guns, and

most of them only wearing loin-cloths, anklets and sandals.'
The Indians gathered round them, hot, weary and thirsty
though they were, and they met the local chief, Santiago, who
next day took them to visit a nearby village. Alfred was
saddened by what he saw:

> Measles and flu epidemics had been raging among the
> Indians and also among many of the Argentines and on
> every side we saw sick people lying on the ground in
> filthy rags, utterly miserable. Their only hope is that a
> witch-doctor may by singing chants, rattling gourds and
> making other unearthly noises, be able to drive away
> the evil spirits that are afflicting them. Many people have
> died and everywhere women were to be seen with their
> hair cut off short, a sign that they have lost some near
> relative.
>
> In the first village we visited I heard for the first time the
> Indian death-wail, and I never wish to hear it again. I
> cannot imagine anything more hopeless or pathetic than to
> see an Indian woman with shorn hair, walking to and fro
> shaking a gourd and wailing in a most uncanny way, thus
> expressing in her way the grief that she feels.
>
> It is so often said by a certain class of people that foreign
> missions are unnecessary and uncalled for: 'Why bother to
> go to the Indians,' they say. 'They are quite happy, they
> hunt, they fish, they live their own life; they are much
> better left alone.' I wish it were possible for such people to
> visit the Indians in their wild state and afterwards to visit
> those at Algarrobal, who have found what it means to have
> a Saviour in Christ Jesus, and are proving from day to day
> to all who see them that there is only one power that can
> uplift mankind, and that is the Gospel of Christ.

After attempting, together with Fitzgerald, to organise a
peace conference between opposing factions of Matacos
(it was a failure as only one party turned up) and giving
medical help to one or two needy people, they set off back to
Algarrobal, arriving at the end of September.

A month later all was ready for the setting up of the new mission, and on October 31st there was a valedictory service in the church at Algarrobal, during which the 'pioneers' knelt at the communion rail while leading Mataco Christians prayed for them and for the new venture. It was a moving occasion, and as Alfred commented, 'Two Mataco evangelists – Rafael and Juan – were going with us and this outreach was seen as the first real attempt of the church at Algarrobal to send some of its members into the regions beyond and to take the good news to their more primitive fellow tribesmen living there. Algarrobal had become a *sending church* and was showing its concern for others.'

The people among whom the mission party settled (after a twelve-day journey with two laden carts) were what anthropologists call 'hunters and gatherers'. The river, with its abundance of fish, supplied much of their food, and Alfred, who had come from a fishing community in England to another so far away, describes their way of life.

At that time they were semi-nomadic and knew practically nothing of agriculture. They lived literally off the land – the men hunting game and catching fish, the women gathering roots, fruits and berries from the forest. They often had hungry spells between seasons, as apart from fruit not much could be stored because of the heat, but on the whole they did very well, with a varied diet. As well as the foods already mentioned, there were carob beans, with which the Chaco forest abounds, and when the rains were good, a certain amount of produce such as maize, beans, pumpkins and melons from their primitive plantations. In winter, when fruit was scarce, the river supplied them with fish.

They had certain skills: in particular the men made spears and bows and arrows, weapons for hunting and nets for fishing. The women made rough clothing and woven bags from vegetable fibre. At this time the men still wore anklets made of ostrich feathers, and had plugs in their ears and painted faces, but gradually western-style shirts and trousers were taking over. They would bring back these sought-after items of clothing from the cane-fields where they went every year for several months to work.

These trips to the cane-fields were for many of the Indians their first contact with the world beyond their villages. Each year hundreds of them would be gathered together by the agents from the plantations. The agents chose local men – often not the traditional chiefs, but younger men who perhaps had a few words of Spanish – to lead the groups, and with plenty of encouragement in the form of maté, sugar, good food and carefully chosen resting-places at night, the straggling crowd would travel two hundred miles or so, often passing Algarrobal on the way, until their place of work was reached. They would return to their villages six months later, enriched with items of gaudy clothing, a few pots and pans, and perhaps even a gun.

Their houses were beehive-shaped, a rough windowless structure of branches covered with grass and weeds, the low doorway the only way of escape from the smoke of the fire. Inside the house there was next to no furniture (an animal hide on the floor for a bed, a lump of wood for a pillow) and string bags hung from the roof to hold any spare clothes or other goods. A sort of socialism prevailed: everyone living and dressing much the same, any food caught or gathered being shared as a matter of course; meat and fish were usually roasted over an open fire and eaten quickly because of the hot climate; carob beans and other fruit were carefully stored.

Native beer was brewed in large quantities, especially from the algarrobo fruit (carob bean), and at the season when the fruits ripened great drinking feasts would be held, with large supplies of beer being brewed in the hollowed out 'bottle trees' and people from other villages being invited to join in. These feasts could lead to violence and even murder on occasion. The other popular communal diversion was the *hutsaj* dance, the men dancing in a circle, arms linked, the music being provided by their voices and the rhythm by the stamping of their feet. At first we missionaries were intrigued by this spectacle, but when later some of the Indians came to understand the truths of the Gospel and were converted, they themselves pointed out that the dances were almost always a prelude to immorality, and they gradually ceased.

These people were animists and believed that sickness and accident were caused by evil spirits. They feared the spirits of the dead, and often the nights could be noisy and frightening to a newcomer with the chanting of the shaman or witch-doctor, the hideous sounds made to scare away spirits, and the incessant wailing of the bereaved. They had no knowledge of God and no name for him.

This last point is taken up by the famous anthropologist, Alfred Metraux, who himself did much research in the Chaco: 'Missionaries have always failed to find the concept of a Supreme Being in the religion of the Chaco Indians.'[13]

At San Andres the missionaries' work was slow and in many ways unrewarding. Indeed, when they first arrived a drinking bout was in progress and co-operation was minimal. The character, too, of these Matacos led to their being generally morose and unresponsive. Another problem was that they were beset by feuds. The Matacos with whom the missionaries settled were the clan known as the Tiger's Children. Six miles away were their deadly enemies, the Storks – known locally as the Colorados, or Reds.

These were the two clans between whom Fitzgerald and others were trying to arrange a peace conference on the missionaries' first visit, following a serious fight some months before in which some Colorados had been killed. This feuding produced an atmosphere of tension among the Indians. It meant that the missionaries, who soon after their arrival were depending on them to help with building work, could not depend on anyone.

Rumours were rife and at any time some word or sign might be given – unknown to them – and all Indians – workmen, washerwomen and hangers-on – would suddenly disappear for no apparent reason. It also meant that the 'Tiger's Children' were very nervous about leaving the village, knowing that the Storks were eager for their vendetta, or revenge, and it was difficult to get them to go on errands, like collecting the mail from an outpost about five miles away. One strong Indian man hid himself under a blanket in the cart and put a small boy to drive in his place, so frightened was he when passing near the Stork's village at that time. He had reason to be, as he was a marked man.

So the missionaries settled in, living at first in rough shelters. There was no privacy. As one of them put it, 'The Indians were accustomed to wandering in and out of each other's houses, and did the same with ours.' So did the insects, as Richard Hunt has vividly described:

> Perhaps the most troublesome foes to the missionary pioneer are the tiny insects and repulsive reptiles. Fleas swarm in their thousands, while jiggers, not content with crawling or biting, penetrate the skin and have to be extracted. If the mosquito curtains are not carefully tucked in at night, as well as mosquitoes the *vinchuca*, a great bedbug, may enter and, finding some exposed part of the body, like the big toe, will sit and fan the member while it sucks the blood. The house is sometimes entered by an army of foraging ants ... Fleas, jiggers, crickets, scorpions, toads, snakes – all flee before these tiny black scavengers. They spring-clean the house.[14]

As well as fencing the land they had been given and the erection of buildings, their main concerns were to provide elementary medical help, schooling and, of course, to share the Gospel. The first permanent house to go up was of mud and wattle, with a zinc roof; soon a dispensary and a school were built of adobes, or sun-dried bricks, the simple worship services taking place for the moment in the school.

Apart from the feud between the clans, there were other difficulties in the early days. One was a mysterious suicide epidemic. In the forest grew a tree whose fruit (*honai*) when ripe was safe to eat, but if unripe and not boiled five times contains a deadly poison. For generations this fact had been known and treated with respect, but now for no apparent reason young teenage girls began eating this fruit, and unless an emetic was given very quickly, they just lay down and died. It seemed to be a violent effort on the evil one's part to resist the coming of the Gospel.

While the epidemic lasted, the missionaries were called out by night and day to try and help. Some they reached in time, and in some cases they were doubtful if the poison had really been taken, but some bright young people of the village perished. The ringleader seemed to be a girl called Monteya who had somehow developed an immunity to the poison herself. She would take other girls off to the *monte* (forest) to eat the fruit, she herself recovering quickly, but her victims suffering and sometimes dying. The whole atmosphere was charged with evil and the sound of death drums and the death-chant filled the night. The witch-doctors tried by their charms to drive away the evil influence, the missionaries prayed and worked, and at last the epidemic waned.

It is perhaps worth mentioning here that Alfred Metraux put forward a theory that a suicide epidemic of this sort could be related to the cessation of the dancing and so, indirectly, to the coming of the Gospel. He suggested that the dance, drinking feasts, etc. were the ritualised means of expressing anger and aggression, and also that, as suicides were the consequence of unfulfilled sexual affairs, the loss of the dance (which legitimised these affairs) could for this reason, too, be a direct causal factor in suicide. However J. H. Palmer in his thesis (1977) points out that contemporary evidence contradicts Metraux, in that the suicide epidemics did not persist, and are not a feature of Indian life today.

The other serious setback was the flood which took place in 1930. The Pilcomayo usually kept to its natural channel, though varying in size from a mere trickle to a raging torrent. But this time it swelled and swelled until it was lapping the top of the bank, and it was soon clear that it would overflow and flood the mission. All movable property was carried to

higher ground and the people followed, soon to see the adobe
mission houses collapsing until only the first-built house was
left, supported by its posts. It was then discovered that the
people and mission property had become stranded on an
island, so everything, including the goats, had to be moved
by hastily constructed rafts. The current was so strong that
the rafts could not be brought back for a second trip, so new
ones had to be made each time. Alfred observed

> Family parties swimming off with their rafts piled high
> with stores of food and household goods, old women,
> young children, all taking their part and swimming along
> merrily. Women struggling along with tremendous loads
> on their backs; some with babies perched on top; some
> vainly endeavouring to drag along goats, who would
> persist in getting themselves mixed up with the surround-
> ing undergrowth; animals, protesting lustily, being tied
> down to the rafts. Men, many of whom seemed to have
> forgotten the very existence of clothes, rushed shouting
> from place to place, and everything seemed in a general
> state of uproar. The situation was serious, and yet from
> time to time there was some very amusing incident, which
> would cause roars of laughter, and on the whole everybody
> seemed to be in good spirits.

Hardly had this move been completed than the river began
to fall, leaving everything covered with a thick layer of mud.
What to do next? Eventually it was decided, because of the
necessity of fresh water, to rebuild on the existing site, but to
use baked bricks instead of adobes, as they would not
dissolve in the event of another flood.

William Everitt, now back from Bolivia, came to San
Andres and with the help of a providential gift from England,
the work was begun. It is hard to pay adequate tribute to
William. His dedication to his Saviour and to the Chaco
Indians was complete; his energy, hard work and crafts-
manship given unstintingly.

The flood proved to be in some ways a turning-point at San

Andres. The rebuilding under William's vigorous lead provided work for large numbers of men who were thus drawn closer to the mission. Every evening a service was held to explain the Gospel to them, and gradually there were converts. By the time the new church was dedicated there were ten of them – three baptised previously, and seven on the day of the dedication.

The church, which used to surprise the visitor coming upon it through the trees by its likeness to an English village church, is described by Bishop Every, who presided at the service: 'There, set off by the graceful forest trees, wisely left standing in their spring greenery, stood a noble red-roofed solid brick church, cruciform and complete with low west-end tower. Our builder had contented himself with a simple design, and the furniture was in harmony, of the best material and excellent workmanship, but still severely simple.' The bishop observed a difference in the people he had visited two years before: 'Now the fire had been kindled in their hearts and there was response.' He rejoiced with them all that 'The Church of the Good Shepherd [as it was named] has started on its career with ten members in its fold.'

11

'The Tobas are on the road!'

At about this time, some very different Indians began to demand the missionaries' attention: the Tobas – the fierce and assertive race who had caused the Franciscans such problems years before. They lived farther downstream, and some of them began coming to San Andres to sell ostrich feathers and to buy things at the store. Seeing the school in progress, they also began bringing their children to share in the benefits brought by the foreigners, though the benefits were of course limited by the different language which they spoke. A succession of Toba deputations began to arrive, asking for a missionary – primarily not, Henry Grubb thought, because they were anxious to hear the Christian message, but because they wanted support in the face of ill-treatment and interference from 'the whites'. The younger men were also anxious for a school. Once they even brought a horse for the hoped-for missionary to ride!

This development caused the old pioneer, Barbrooke Grubb, to write shortly before his death, rejoicing: 'We have long been drawn to them, and they seem to have been in a wonderful way drawn to us. The fierce, hated Tobas . . . truly it is remarkable . . . . it is of God.'[15]

They looked amazing, the Tobas: tall, dignified, some in traditional dress including feathered head-dress, long hair, beads and bushy anklets of ostrich-feathers; some in a weird collection of army tunics and other Western finery; one, despite the heat, in a complete airman's leather combination suit which he had picked up somewhere. Greetings took place when they arrived, each chief going up to the missionary in turn, and, with his face very close, letting off the 'click-clacks' of the Toba language like a machine-gun.

Alfred had seen them before. He remembered vividly the

thrill of the words heard once in his early days at Algarrobal: 'The Tobas are on the road!' Sure enough that very day he had seen his first Toba, striding through the mission compound as if he owned the place, and soon, while the scared Matacos kept well out of sight, hundreds of them, tall and proud, had come streaming past, on their way to the canefields. Now, two years later, Alfred was chosen to answer their call for a mission. During their visits to San Andres, services were arranged for them with a Mataco who had married a Toba attempting to interpret into Toba. It was noticeable how they would stampede for the front seats as soon as the bell rang – unlike the Matacos who sat shyly at the back.

On the question of Mataco shyness, Alfred observed this often infuriating characteristic – a paralysing timidity, *ofwun*.

Girls in school if asked a question will cover their mouths, or, if they answer, do so very softly so the teacher cannot possibly hear. Women and girls who may have sweet voices cannot pluck up courage to sing. People sent with messages are sometimes too shy to give them. One day a young man walked twenty miles to tell us that his brother had been bitten by a rattlesnake, but when he arrived was unable to get the message out. He hung around the store, made one or two small purchases, and only plucked up courage to tell us why he had come, several hours later when it was almost too late.

Ofwun affects the Lord's work quite seriously. Discussions fall flat as no one will answer a question, let alone summon up the courage to ask one. One preacher was discovered to have given up taking services. Why? He had lost his hymn-book and was too shy to ask to borrow one!

Witnessing, too, becomes very hard when people are so diffident. Curiously, the trait disappears when the Indians speak Spanish. Thus children who refuse to sing in Mataco will simply bawl out choruses if they are taught them in Spanish.

But the Tobas were not shy. In May 1929 Henry and Alfred set out to visit them, leaving Colin Smith and William Everitt holding the fort at San Andres. Near the small white settlement of Sombrero Negro, where the Tropic of Capricorn meets the Pilcomayo, a large crowd of Tobas welcomed them. As Henry recalled:

> We were never left alone for a moment. Crowds of Tobas, on foot and mounted, came with us everywhere. Everyone wanted to shake us by the hand, and there was shouting and singing all the time. We didn't understand a word of the language, and as we listened to the weird conglomeration of sounds, we wondered if we ever would. Our Mataco companion was scared stiff, and kept between the two of us as being the safest place.

In November 1930, Alfred Leake and Alec Sanderson, son of a long-serving missionary in Paraguay, set off to start the Toba mission. Sanderson left almost at once and went back to Paraguay as his father died, and his place was taken by a recent recruit to SAMS, George Freestone. The Toba venture was very much harder than at San Andres. For one thing, no one spoke the language at the start, whereas Mataco was already well known. Fortunately one Indian spoke both languages, and another Toba and a little Spanish, so they were able to help.

It was a complex language to learn, sounding at first like a jumble of clicking sounds. Gradually Alfred learnt to speak it, preaching his first Toba sermon on March 22nd, 1931. He was saddened though that his congregation laughed when he spoke of the Cross, laughter being a common response to physical suffering among the Indians. It brought home to him the width of the gulf to be bridged, and later he realised that he should have started his preaching with something closer to their experience – God the Good Spirit, as the spirit world was already real to them.

On the other hand, one old chief commented, after being told something of the love of God, 'We have often heard about our Father. We have looked for him. Sometimes we have been told that he was in a certain place and we have gone to that place but we have not found him. We had no one to trust, but now in these days we come to you. Our homes are far distant but what of that, you are truly our Father's servants. We hear his words and we believe in him.' These were no idle worlds; this man had travelled 130 miles to hear the Gospel preached.

In 1931 Henry Grubb visited the new Toba mission; he found mosquitoes – lots; buildings – nothing much as yet. Within half a mile several hundred Indians had gathered, anxious to be near the mission. The settlement stood on a green and shady part of the river bank with abundant grass and bright wild flowers, and ancient overshadowing trees.

Noticeable at once was the importance of horses to the Tobas. Outside the village their horses grazed, the bell round the neck of the leader or 'bell-mare' sounding gently as she moved. The Tobas, both men and women, are splendid horsemen, and as another visitor many years later observed, 'To see one of the young girls with nothing but a bit of string as a bit and snaffle and a blanket for a saddle, is an unforgettable sight.' Their livestock is a topic of absorbing interest to the Tobas, and one missionary reckoned that a good half of the conversations he held with them were about animals of one sort and another.

Another source of keen enjoyment to the Tobas was their hockey game, which only men and boys played. There weren't many rules, the goal was a heap of bushes and a small wooden ball was used. The players stripped off all their clothes and adorned themselves with belts of metal discs which jangled as they ran. They painted their faces and bodies with black paint or soot, and, to give strength and speed to their legs, they punctured them with sharpened ostrich bones so that the blood ran down. They had a notion that piercing the skin with the appropriate object would impart to them the required attribute: a jaguar's bone for ferocity, the bone of a wild pig for skill in keeping hidden, and so on. A group of Tobas playing hockey was a truly fearsome sight.

Henry commented, too:

> The Tobas are enthusiastic dancers and nightly the sound
> of their dancing and singing lulled us to sleep, or other-
> wise. The women tattooed their faces, producing a gro-
> tesque appearance, and in many other ways the Tobas
> were more primitive than the Matacos. The tribe was
> much feared by the few Argentine squatters of the district,
> since it was not many years since a local rising of Tobas
> had completely wiped out one of the little forts established
> by the military to control them, killing every soldier.

Henry stayed for two months, and mastered enough of the
Toba language himself to help with organising and typing
the lists of Toba words Alfred had collected. Services were
being held and were very popular, with an average of 250
adults attending each Sunday. They would come considerable distances, usually arriving on Saturday to be sure of
being in time, camping round their fires overnight. As Alfred
commented, 'We are aware of many imperfections. The
services have to be held in the open air where the usual
disturbances are so apt to take place; then we have no
musical instrument and the noise we make when we try to
sing is terrible.'

And so they persevered. George Freestone wrote home,
describing how 'the cold south wind, playing with the flaps
of the mission tent, occasionally reveals a glimpse of a
head bowed over a desk of rude structure. It is the missionary
at language study.' He describes, too, the constant
interruptions:

'My wife has been bitten by a poisonous spider. She is in
great pain. Would the "elder brother" come and bring
medicine?'

Next an Argentine settler: 'Would the mission like to buy a
cow?' The washergirl needs advice; the workmen mudding
the new building need watching; the kitchen boy cannot yet
be left alone with the bread which is rising in an old biscuit
tin near the fire. A party of Chunupi – another tribe with

another language – arrives from across the river. And so life goes on. A few weeks later a local policeman calls.

'But the Indians did not build these houses?' He nods in the direction of the new store and dispensary buildings and towards the partly-built missionaries' house.

'Oh yes, they did – why not?' He is surprised and impressed.

In November 1931 George Freestone left, and Olive Leake, Alfred's sister, came out from Algarrobal where she had been helping as a nurse for the last two years, and started 'making things considerably more comfortable and home-like'. She was self-effacing and quiet, like Alfred, and a kindly and efficient nurse.

Christmas was busy, with four hundred people packing the new school building for the first lantern service, and a sports day on Boxing Day when huge crowds attended, and, as Alfred described, 'It was a treat to see old Choliqui (the oldest of the chiefs) dressed only in a skirt, belt and head-dress running alongside the younger ones, some of whom sported full Argentine suits and even shoes and socks.' The children were thrilled with gifts from children in Buenos Aires, a custom which was kept up year after year.

With John Arnott, Alfred Cox and later Bill Price joining the Toba team, Alfred went home on furlough in 1932. While there he became engaged to Dorothy, a pretty girl with laughing eyes whom he had known since they were both children at the East Runton village school. He came back to find the Bolivian-Paraguayan war raging, a war which was to see the land across the river transferred from Bolivia to Paraguay.

As he reported back to England, 'For months we have had Bolivian soldiers opposite us and of course never expected to see the Paraguayans up so far as this. The Indians are allowed to move freely on both sides of the river and at present the Paraguayan soldiers are being very kind to them.' He went on though to point out the gravity of the war, the tremendous loss of lives and homes involved, and to ask for prayer for the bereaved and homeless of both countries.

In July 1934 a great event took place at the Toba mission – Dorothy's arrival and the wedding. Dorothy had spent a year at the Redcliffe Missionary Training College in London, and then sailed out on a cargo boat to join Alfred. The Archdeacon for the Republics of the River Plate met her at Buenos Aires and accompanied her on the long, dusty train journey to Juarez, the small station some fifty miles from Sombrero Negro. (A railway line had been newly built from Formosa to Embarcacion, parallel to and between the rivers Bermejo and Pilcomayo, an improvement in communications which made life easier for the missionaries and others, but which also hastened the inevitable urbanisation of the Chaco Indians.)

Here Alfred, accompanied by Henry Grubb in his indomitable Ford car, 'Susan', which he had acquired in 1931, met her at two in the morning. They were married there by the civil registrar: 'When I nudge you, say "si",' Alfred primed her. She was so excited she overdid it: 'si, si!'

But the real celebrations were to come. First a bumpy fifty-mile ride in Henry's car, the journey's end heralded by a bright banner stretched across the path from tree to tree: 'Welcome, ray of sunshine!' (a reference to instructions given to Dorothy by the mission headquarters in London: 'Go out and be a ray of sunshine to them all.')

Then, as Alfred recorded,

We were met by hundreds of Tobas, many of whom had been playing their old native game of hockey and so were well painted and feathered, and after spending a few hectic moments in a seething mass of hot and dusty humanity, having our hands shaken up and down like pump-handles, we were informed that we must climb into the old mission four-wheeler which was standing by gaily decorated with coloured pieces of cloth, bearing messages of welcome in three languages, and be dragged into the mission. This we did and amid the shouts and laughter of the Indians we were pulled along at no mean speed right into the compound. I shall never forget the sight, the men as they pulled away with a will on the four-wheeler, the waving head-dresses, the painted faces, the women and children running, laughing excitedly, the horsemen (who included some of the missionaries) riding bareback in a real Indian fashion, the flying banners of welcome.

The simple religious ceremony took place that day, and Dorothy settled down with Alfred to her new home and work. They had wanted to share their marriage with the Tobas, as this was the first Christian wedding to be seen among them. The hope was to set a pattern for the Indians to follow, and Alfred and Dorothy were happy for this to be so. Alfred Tompkins, now ordained, took the service in English for Dorothy's sake, but Bill Price carefully translated everything into Toba so that the watching Indians could understand the meaning of the vows and of all that was said.

In fact church weddings never really caught on among the Indians, although once they were registered as Argentine citizens, a civil wedding was required. (In this connection, it was recorded in a SAMS annual report of the 1930s relating to Algarrobal that 'Permission has been granted by the Argentine government to register our communicants as citizens . . . so they are now being civilly married and are taking their place as men and women of the Republic, and can no longer be treated as savages or wild beasts of the forest.')

12

Years of Fruitfulness and Growth

The 1930s were years of fruitfulness and growth in the church of the Argentine Chaco. Take the Toba mission first.

In March 1934 Alfred wrote home to England that after three and a half years' work among the Tobas, although the atmosphere in the village was far less heathen and the quality of some individuals' lives was certainly improved, not one Toba had yet responded to the call of Jesus Christ. He was aware that 'the very knowledge which they have gained from us (in the school) will be a snare to them if they are not brought to Christ.'

In response to earnest prayer, the situation soon changed dramatically. First, some of the Toba men decided, on their own initiative, to build a 'prayer hut'. And soon after that, in November, the first definite conversions took place. First came Nagadi, one of the most difficult people on the mission. He was followed, in the space of about four weeks, by sixteen more young men, all of whom prayed, confessing their sins, claiming salvation through Christ and asking for the indwelling presence and help of the Holy Spirit.

One of these was the son of a leading local witch-doctor, another a boy who eighteen months previously had stolen some cloth and then tried deceitfully, using his new writing skills, to prove that it had been given him in exchange for work. Sadly, many of these later fell away, but this was only the beginning, and during the next six months over 250 people came pouring in, both from the mission and from nearby villages where itinerant preaching was being done, professing conversion and clamouring for admission to the instruction class.

Was this a movement of the Holy Spirit, or did all these people come forward because it had suddenly become the popular thing to do? Alfred thought the answer was possibly *both*. A 'group consensus' having been reached, a whole cultural group, as frequently happens when pagan societies first hear the Gospel, was turning to Christ.

In one nearby village, where previously nobody had seemed very interested in the Gospel, suddenly, almost as a body, the whole village professed faith. Each week they travelled the five miles to MET (Mision El Toba) for the class, often staying several days, camping round their fires, in order to attend the prayer-meetings and Sunday services. Soon they asked to borrow tools and built a prayer-hut in their village, where daily, night and morning, they gathered for prayer. Their leader, and the one instrumental in the building of the prayer-hut, was a man who three years earlier Alfred had had to hand over to the police for the murder of an Argentine.

In the midst of this joyful burgeoning of spiritual life, a baby boy was born to Alfred and Dorothy. He was born at MET, with the able midwifely help of Alfred's sister, Olive, and was called David.

By the end of 1935, Alfred was able to report that although some enquirers had fallen away, many were remaining faithful. As he commented, 'They have passed through the temptations and pull of the heathen world only known to those who are the first of a tribe to seek to follow Christ after countless generations of heathenism.' The women were particularly unresponsive, he observed, although one, Dechenai, seemed truly converted.

Another hopeful development took place in 1935 – the opening of Mision Pilaga, among the southern and more remote Tobas who had actually been the first to send a deputation to San Andres asking for a mission. There were difficulties, largely due to the fact that these Tobas lived in a military zone where Argentine forts were dotted about every few leagues. Clashes first with the military and then with the Chunupi among whom they attempted to settle, led to their moving to MET. The area could not possibly sustain a population suddenly increased from five hundred to a thousand, and so in October Bill Price and John Arnott set off to start a new mission settlement with them, on the edge of a reedy lagoon some twenty-five miles to the south-east of MET.

Alfred and Dorothy and Olive were not left alone when they went. They were joined briefly by Leslie Harwood who had been working in Bolivia. He spent his time on an interesting project: altering the spelling in the version of Mark's Gospel recently translated by Alfred and Bill Price, to bring it more into line with Spanish. As Alfred explained,

> Spanish is, of course, taught to some extent in the school, side by side with Toba. The difference between the partly English spelling of the Toba reading material which we have prepared and the Spanish readers has caused some confusion, and it has been difficult to explain to Argentine visitors that we do not teach English to the Indians, when they see in our Toba translations letters which are rarely if ever seen in Spanish!

We can see what he meant:

> Old spelling: Hataki hawoko kadakataka mui onagaiyaka
> New spelling: Jetaqui jauoco cadacataca mi onogayaca.

Another helper joined Alfred and Dorothy this year: Alfred Tebboth, soon to be known by his second name Thomas (Tomás), as there were too many Alfreds around. Son of a postman, he had arrived in the Chaco in 1930 at the age of 21. He was impressed by what he saw on his first arrival at Algarrobal:

> It was strange to meet the Matacos. They spoke very slowly. They all came rushing to church and after church they could get rations from the store. I was amazed to see that one of them, Moises, could drive the car [Alfred Leake had taught him to be both driver and mechanic]; it was all very well run. There was a big wooden bungalow, 'the white house', where Mr Grubb lived, and 'the vicarage',

surrounded by lovely ferns, for the Tompkins family. There was the school, where Mr Grubb taught, with Indians helping him.

Tomás didn't stay at Algarrobal, but was sent to Bolivia, where he mastered Guarani and stayed until the mission was forced to close. It was then that he came to join the Leakes at MET. Gifted with languages, he struggled in the heat and absence of privacy to learn Toba – 'There were Indians in the bedrooms – everywhere!' One of his first tasks was typing out the Toba version of Mark's Gospel which Alfred and Bill Price had translated, ready for printing in Buenos Aires. In fact Tomás Tebboth's mastery of Toba became so good that a Spanish-Toba dictionary which he worked at over the years was published in 1943 by the Institute of Anthropology of the National University of Tucuman.

And so the work went on. A visitor in 1936 was told by the Tobas, 'Lucaicachigui the-tall-one [Alfred Leake], he knows our language and understands us, and so does Lucaina, the-tall-one (Mrs Leake), and Jadiocoli, the-small-unseen-one (Miss Leake).' This visitor described the mission station El Toba hidden away in primeval forest on the steep banks of the Pilcomayo, the prayer-huts which had recently been built, the fishermen going off together in the morning and coming back at the end of the day with their catch strung up and hung around their dark shiny bodies like a girdle.

'And at sunset the youngsters dive into the Pilcomayo and swim with glee, yelling and shouting and racing wild around the sand-banks.' She noticed that although the Gospel was taking root among these people, 'the charm of El Toba is that her people still live in their primitive state. Families sit squatted on goatskins in front of their huts, partially naked, boiling fish or broiling it on stakes over crackling fires.' She also noted how one convert, 'Tiger', appeared proudly on his wedding day in a baseball outfit and army hat brought back from the cane-fields, blissfully unconscious of its incongruity.

Life among the Tobas for the Leakes and their helpers was certainly never dull. Like all missionary work, it had its joys

and sadnesses. Reading through Alfred's voluminous records, a kaleidoscopic picture is built up, of animists who
believed that every sickness and accident was caused by evil
spirits. This was why nights among them were so noisy – a
constant cacophony of rattling gourds had to be kept up to
frighten the spirits away. (The witch-doctor, understand-
ably, didn't like Alfred Leake: 'Why don't you bewitch him?'
someone asked. 'I can't,' was the reply. 'Every night his spirit
goes up to his God.' In other words, Alfred fell peacefully
asleep!)

When someone died, their spirit was supposed to roam
abroad with evil effects. This belief led to their sometimes
burying a dying person before death actually occurred – a
way of scotching the evil spirit before it left the body. Once,
when a dying woman he had been tending disappeared,
Alfred, following the indication of another Toba woman,
came upon a big bonfire in the forest, and beside it, in the
blazing sun, sewn up in an Indian string-bag of the sort used
for corpses, the desperately ill woman with terrified eyes,
cries of pain and terror issuing from her parched lips. Alfred
persuaded the people involved to move her into the shade,
and two trusted evangelists came and watched over her until
the inevitable end came. But at least she was spared being
burnt alive.

The ways of the heathen Tobas and the change wrought by
Christ were clearly exemplified in an old Toba warrior who
was known as Apagaliquitela (Flat Ear) because he had
taken on the nickname of an Argentinian settler he had killed
who did have a slightly deformed ear. Flat Ear was one of the
chiefs, and he was a character. Small and energetic, when
work was in progress he would be seen jumping around
excitedly, shouting out orders. One day Alfred heard a shot
ring out, only to discover that it was Flat Ear who had 'shot
the demon' in the chest of a man whom Alfred had been
trying to treat for pneumonia, thereby killing the patient as
well.

Flat Ear had a sickly son known as Kunim (Skunk). One
day poor Skunk became seriously ill and it seemed that not

much could be done. Shortly after this, Flat Ear came and borrowed the mission wheelbarrow. At first Alfred thought nothing of it, but then he began to wonder. He rushed up to the village and found, as he feared, Skunk on the barrow, covered with a blanket and tied down with thongs. His father was about to bury him alive in the forest to prevent his spirit escaping and doing harm. The situation was averted, and three days later Skunk died peacefully.

Old Flat Ear eventually turned to Christ, taking the name Abraham, and when he himself became mortally ill he staggered from a neighbouring village to the house of Salomon, one of the leading Christians at the Toba mission. Early one morning Salomon's wife heard Abraham praying, committing himself to his Lord. She made up the fire for him and then, his prayer finished, he drew his blanket around him and curled up like a tired child, never to wake again in this world. No fear of demons now, no wailing of witch-doctors; simply trust in the One he had come to know and love.

The witch-doctor's, or shaman's, healing efforts were based on the rattling of gourds, and also on the apparent extraction of perhaps a stick, a stone or a beetle which was supposed to be causing the illness. As the missionaries came to be trusted more than the witch-doctors, a new difficulty arose for them with the belief that they had supernatural powers against sickness. When healing didn't always occur, the Indian was tempted to become disillusioned.

The poor missionaries did their best, and as Alfred recalled, 'A terrific amount of time was spent poring over medical books trying to diagnose and then treat the various complaints.' In particular, TB and malaria were very prevalent, measles and whooping-cough were often killers among the children, and snakebites and the bites of the cannibal fish (piranha) in the river were common hazards. So was chagas, a disease transmitted by the vinchuca beetle, which affects the heart.

This belief in the omnipotence of the missionaries had gradually to be corrected, and a better understanding was

reflected in the changing names given to them, from 'Cadet'a
– Our Father', the name which they later gave to God, to 'our
other', 'our flesh-brother', and once, to Alfred's joy, when he
happened to be ill and the Christians were praying for him,
'our suckling-companion' (one who suckled at the same
breast).

One highlight which Alfred Leake remembers was the first
celebration of Holy Communion among the Tobas.

> It was a wonderful service, and the way in which these
> primitive people grasped the significance of the sacrament
> amazed me. It was something which could so easily lend
> itself to superstition. It was at that service, taken some
> seven or eight years after the commencement of the work,
> that the very first offering was taken. We had of course
> taught them about giving, and they responded mag-
> nificently. There wasn't much money about, but those
> who had none gathered firewood or did some other odd job
> to earn a little cash. There was one old man, who just
> before the offertory was taken, called out to let us know he
> had left his at home. His offering when he fetched it was the
> equivalent of one day's pay for an Indian.

With two small children now – Cristina was born in 1937 –
Alfred and Dorothy carried on cheerfully. As well as basic
medical work, teaching and evangelism, they developed an
important role as intermediaries in the perpetual squabbles
between the Indians and the settlers. One Sunday morning,
as the Tobas were streaming out of the bamboo and palm
church after the service, the peace was shattered by the
shouting and gesticulating of an old woman, 'Queduk,
queduk!' (Tiger, tiger!) The men looked first nonplussed and
then all agog.

'Where is it?'

'Just over there, in the fenced-off part where the horses
are!'

The men rushed home for their guns and soon a shot rang
out . . . and then another and another. 'There must be a lot of

tigers around this morning,' thought the puzzled missionaries. Eventually the truth came out. There hadn't been a tiger, but 'white men's cows broke into the fenced area and were eating our animals' food'. Five cows had been shot.

What were the missionaries to do? They could imagine the indignation of the settlers: 'So this is how the Indians behave when they come out of church!' This was the sort of thing which, in the past, had called for police reinforcements, or even the military. The missionaries acted quickly, informing the owners of the cattle and the police what had happened. Most important, they managed to persuade the Tobas to offer a recompense in the form of large quantities of algarrobo beans from their bumper harvest, to which they added an old gun. Alfred thought that this was probably the first time in history that Argentine squatters had received recompense for animals killed by Indians, and he thanked God that his Spirit was at work, bringing peace.

13
Regino's Dream

While the Tobas were responding to the Good News, the work among the Matacos was continuing at San Andres. The year 1931 saw the baptism of the first three converts and the conversion of Isakis, a notable witch-doctor or shaman. Previously 'arrayed in head-dress and feathers, with many empty sardine-tins suspended from his waist, his face smeared with charcoal and other filth, his heart as hard as flint and his life as dark as the night around him and the powers whose aid he sought', he affirmed that now he was God's child. Gradually the believers began to pray to their newly-found Father: 'We have been like wild beasts wandering in the forest, but your servants found us and your words entered our hearts. Now we desire to be your children.'

Through these new Christians the Gospel was carried in various directions during the 1930s, particularly to the villages along the banks of the Pilcomayo River. Most of the subsequent growth was accomplished by Indian evangelists under God, rather than by missionaries. Like their patron, St Andrew, once they had come to know the risen Christ, these Matacos were eager to introduce others to him.

One of the first converts was Chifwoj-nus (cicada beetle-nose), who took the name of Regino at baptism. He was a good worker and became a carpenter, taught by William Everitt. One morning he came along to the missionaries in some distress:

'I have had a dream and I don't know what it means. I was going out of the mission here when I met a friend. "Where are you going?" he asked me.

'I am going to visit the villages of some of my own people to tell them of the truths we have learned here,' I replied.

'"I'll come with you," he said. Then I awoke. What can it mean?'

'Regino, you interpret this dream for yourself. Go and talk to your friend about it,' they advised.

In due course both Indians returned. 'We have decided that God was speaking to us through this dream, and telling us what he wants us to do. We are going to start travelling to the nearby villages, taking the message of Jesus to our people,' they said.

And so they did, and gradually others joined them. Their reception varied. In some places they were well received; in others the dogs were turned loose on them. In one village where a drinking feast was in progress when they arrived, Regino had a knife put to his chest:

'"Go away and stop this foolish talk, or I kill you," I was told. But I just kept on quietly talking about the word of God, and at last the knife was withdrawn.'

The immediate result of these evangelistic itinerations was unexpected: many of the hearers wanted to learn more, and so large numbers of Indians left their homes and moved to San Andres, where the population doubled itself in no time, until, the food supplies running out, they had to leave again. But some stayed long enough to find their way to God and put their trust in him, among them a young man called Fwapo-chalaj, or Black Shoulder, who on baptism took the name of Mariano.

Alfred Leake remembers that

The first time I saw Mariano was in 1928 or '29. I was sitting at my table when I looked up and saw a lad outside whom I had never seen before. He was just gazing round, taking everything in, and seemed so interested. I had a talk with him and found that he had come from over the river, where his people lived. This was his first visit and he was obviously impressed. After a good look round, he returned home, but later came back with all his family. They settled down and built their huts and Fwapo-Chalaj was soon in school and paying a bit more attention than many of the other children. He did well and was soon reading simple words and eventually became a good scholar. He was honest, too, as was proved at the time of the flood at San Andres, when he rescued the cash-box from the store and brought it proudly to us later, with all the cash intact.

Like Regino, Mariano became a good carpenter under the guiding hand of William Everitt. He was outstanding in many ways and as he grew up began to do evangelistic work locally, so that when people in the Desmontes and Santa Teresa district asked for someone to go and teach them, Mariano was the obvious choice. It was the area from which Rosita, his wife, had originally come. He and Rosita overcame many sorrows and difficulties, and such was his influence that although he was not, nor ever wished to be, the village chief, gradually matters for decision came to be referred to him, and regularly he brought forward new converts for baptism.

Many years later he was one of the first Indians to be ordained. The village became known for the honesty of its inhabitants and Mariano has always been widely respected by whites and Indians alike. Gradually neighbouring villages – Alto de la Sierra, Pozo Mulato, Maria Cristina – wanted Christian teaching, too, and Mariano was able to send people whom he had taught, to teach them. As Henry Grubb commented, 'All these centres and more grew out of Desmontes, and none had ever had a resident missionary, though we had visited them all from time to time. How much grew out of that dream of Regino's!'

Another small mission, El Yuto, some fifteen miles downstream from San Andres, was founded by Colin Smith, who went there in January 1936 at the request of the Yuto Indians. The mission diary from El Yuto, covering the period when the missionaries lived there, from 1936 to 1939, has been preserved. It gives a vivid picture of the pressures and joys which missionaries and Indians shared.

Starting with Colin Smith's exploratory visit from San Andres in January 1936, together with two evangelists, Fidel and Juan José, it describes the movement of several local chiefs with their people to the chosen site about two hundred metres from the Pilcomayo, each chief selecting several of his young men to help with building a mission house, the arrangement being that they shared a big pot of food each day, and had the promise of a piece of cloth when the building was completed. The diary records that about forty Yuto Indians had been members of the enquirers' class at San Andres, so these formed the nucleus of an enquirers' class at Yuto from the first. By July all the chiefs and nearly two hundred of their people had been dealt with on profession of repentance and faith.

In August 1936, when Colin Smith had gone back to San Andres, Ernest Panter, who had spent five years in Bolivia, came to El Yuto with his young wife, Marjorie, known as Timmy, and their first child, Ruth. Theirs was a romantic story. Timmy was twenty years younger than Ernest, and had first met him when she was 14 and he was the curate at the church where she had been converted in the Sunday school in England – Christchurch, Claughton, Birkenhead. Ernest came from a well-to-do family. He had been a naval officer and his father had been a naval chaplain. When Timmy was 18, Ernest left Claughton and went to work as a missionary in Bolivia with SAMS. Timmy concentrated on nursing training, treasuring the letters that he wrote. Once, at a prayer-conference at Swanwick, she overheard two people talking together: 'Isn't it sad about Mr Panter?' they were saying. They had no idea how deeply I was attached to him.

'What has happened?' I asked, my heart in my mouth.

'It was in the local paper,' they replied. 'He has died of fever in Argentina.'

'I was due to take part in the service that evening by testimony and song, so I went up to my room and just cast myself upon the Lord. I sang with great power that night, but it wasn't easy. A few days later a telegram arrived, "News definitely untrue. Writing."'

Ernest proposed to Timmy by letter, and in 1934 when he was home on furlough, they were married. They went out to

Argentina together soon afterwards, first to Algarrobal and then to El Yuto. They had eight children altogether, of whom the first three, Ruth, Grace and Philip, were born in Argentina.

While the Panters were at El Yuto, there was constant tension between various factions, as for example when friction between the Indians and the Paraguayan soldiers on the other side of the river due to the alleged complicity of the former in cattle-running for Argentine settlers, led to an Indian being shot while fishing. Similarly, a year later a white settler was shot by the Paraguayans on suspicion of stealing cattle on the river bank opposite the mission, and in the same month a young married woman, Lanaya, was shot by the Thokotas (the 'Storks') and killed while out gathering algarrobo beans.

In July 1937 there was another unpleasant incident when four Indians crossed the river to sell hens to the Paraguayans who had asked for them. Later one of the Indians came running back alone, without his skirt and bloodstained from head to waist, carrying a gun and shouting, 'I kill him. He kill my father.'

It seemed that the Paraguayans had told Siyakates to go back and procure some women and they would give him a gun. He refused, whereupon one of the soldiers pointed his gun at another Indian, Akonkos, the father of Siyakates, so close that Akonkos struck the muzzle with his hand. He then turned away and was shot through the back of the neck.

The soldiers then attacked Siyakates, who wrested a gun from one of them and shot him dead. The authorities dealt leniently with Siyakates, who clearly was not the guilty party, and the Panters as always gave practical and spiritual support. The diary records that the ages of the Paraguayan who was killed and his friend were 16 and 15 respectively.

Meanwhile the regular life of the mission progressed. As Mrs Panter remembers:

We lived in a hut with just one room and a small extension for beds, and a veranda where we usually ate. There was plenty of food, including excellent fish from the river. Little Ruth learnt the Mataco language very easily and she used to translate for us. We sang choruses: '*Hap ihóye, hap ihóye . . .*' ('When he cometh, when he cometh . . .') to the accompaniment of a small harmonium sent up to us from Buenos Aires. The Indians loved singing. We had a daily service. Every evening at five a bell was rung, and the Indians came trailing single file from their huts nearby. They were being well taught in the Scriptures and were eager for teaching. Many were born again and were showing signs of new life in this way. My husband quickly learnt the Mataco language. He loved the Indians, and they loved 'Mista Panta' as they called him, dearly. We taught the children reading, writing and arithmetic; we taught them in Spanish and Mataco.

In December 1936 seven professing Christians from El Yuto were baptised at San Andres and in April 1937 nineteen more. The Indians built themselves a simple church which was completed on May 26th: it had a grass roof, mud floor, slightly raised sanctuary, Lord's table, vestry and no furniture! The next day Bishop Every came and held his first confirmation service there after dedicating the new church. Sixteen men and ten women were presented, their number including seven married couples. The church was packed, many having to stand outside.

During this time, something rather wonderful happened. It is a complicated story, and is connected with the long-standing feud already mentioned between the two factions of Matacos, the Hayajles or Tiger's Children and the Thokotas or Storks. A young man from a village some thirty miles away and on the other side of the river was shot dead by the Storks while walking home with a friend after singing carols at San Andres. At once a raiding party from his village, painted and dressed for war, attacked the Stork village, but found it deserted, as two women had given warning of the attack. Only one little girl, Silokitaya (Not Alone), had been left behind, and her they took as hostage.

Soon these people moved from their village across the river and came to join their fellow tribesmen who were gathering round the new mission at El Yuto, and soon after this the Storks attacked again, killing a woman who was out in the forest, gathering food – this was Lanaya, whose death has already been mentioned.

At once El Yuto was in uproar, with the men demanding immediate reprisals, and it says much for the influence of the Gospel that Ernest Panter and the other Christians managed to dissuade them. Instead it was decided to send an evangelist to the Storks from El Yuto. The provision of this evangelist was remarkable, too.

There was a family living in El Yuto, who had arrived not very long before. The man had lived in exile for many years, as he himself had killed a man and lived in fear of the vendetta. Hearing of the good news which was being preached at El Yuto, he had come back with his family and decided to follow a very old Mataco custom of making payment for the death of the man he had killed. All was eventually settled and the family became Christians, their son Andreas showing a particularly good grasp of the truth and soon becoming an effective preacher himself. He was the one who offered to go with the good news of Christ to the Storks, and he and his wife and family settled with them at a place called Carmen, where gradually a church was established.

These Indians, the Storks, having always lived deep in the forest, had had little contact with civilisation. They were the only known fire-walkers in the Chaco, and in appearance were very ill-kempt. However several of them became very real Christians, eager to reach out to their neighbours with the faith.

And what of Silokitaya, the little girl who had been captured? She too went home to her village and eventually married and became the mother of a young man called José Daniel who later became the pastor in charge of a small church on the riverside at a place called Pozo Algarrobo. So ended the long feud between the Storks and their enemies.

One of the results of the preaching of the Gospel among the Indians of South America has undoubtedly been the establishing of tribal peace, and even relations between Indians and Argentines are much improved.

The Panters had to leave suddenly in 1939 owing to the health problems – notably eye infections – of the children, and for a time their place was taken by another outstanding missionary, the Rev. William White, and his wife, who had been working at San Andres and at its substation, San Martin. Then when health problems forced them to go to another mission in the Salta province, the work at Yuto was continued under the leadership of Ernesto and Nazaria, two Matacos from San Andres.

Since then the little church at Yuto has had its ups and downs – as when, after a period with many conversions, a group under the leadership of one of their number called Solito, moved three miles away and separated themselves completely from the Christian nucleus in the village. Later again, an evangelist from Yuto called Noe began visiting these people at their request, and holding open-air services for them with the support of the Yuto church.

Despite long periods each year when many families left Yuto for work in the cane-fields and elsewhere, the church and the school struggled on, several of the young men trained as evangelists, and even some of the women have been eager to learn and to pass on what they know. It was evangelists from Yuto who first took the Gospel to nearby Puesto Garcia in the 1960s, and one of them, Bartolomé, made his home among the people there. So in this secluded village on the green banks of the Pilcomayo, the Gospel continued to bear fruit until, recently, Yuto was washed away by floods.

14
Along the Bermejo

Let's leave the Pilcomayo now and go back to Algarrobal.
Here during the 1930s and '40s were Henry Grubb, mission
superintendent since Richard Hunt and Dr Edward Bernau
retired, Alfred Tompkins and his wife and his sister Dorothy,
and Yolande Royce, a very competent nurse. Also during the
1930s several new missionaries arrived, who after a spell of
language study at Algarrobal went on to small outposts of the
developing work.

According to Guilfredo Ibarra, Richard Hunt's retirement
in 1929 was precipitated by three urgent letters from his
long-suffering wife: 'Come back home.' Two hundred and
thirty people filled the church to say goodbye to him, and
'Martin and Juaquincito gave splendid testimony to the
great work of Mr Hunt.'

The church at Algarrobal had made excellent progress:
seven Indians had been licensed as lay-evangelists and were
teaching, preaching and visiting the surrounding villages;
the four Gospels and the Book of Acts had been translated
into Mataco, and a monthly service was being held in
Spanish for the Argentines who came for medical help.

Algarrobal lay on the road which led from the Gran Chaco
to 'civilisation' – epitomised at that time by the railway
station at Embarcacion, and among the groups of Indians
who would pass through annually on their way to the
cane-fields was a group of some four hundred Matacos led by
their chief, Feliz Paz. Over a period of many years he asked
Henry about the possibility of a mission being started among
his people who lived about a hundred miles to the south-east,
and eventually one pouring wet day Henry, riding his famous
white mule and accompanied by an Indian guide, nick-
named Beans, set off on an exploratory trip (the nickname

stemmed from the similarity of the boy's name, Angyates, to that of a wild bean, Angyatas).

In 1933 it was decided to go ahead and start a mission, and some weeks later Henry Grubb, Bertram Treanor and Alfred Cox set out to found, on the edge of a lagoon set among thick forest and cactus growth, the settlement which became known as San Patricio. The site, once cleared, was beautiful, and perfect for a mission – an area of higher land overlooking the lagoon which provided both necessary water and fish. Spoonbills, cranes and other water-birds glided gracefully over the lake.

Soon the peace was shattered not only by sounds of building work and the arrival of Feliz Paz and large numbers of Indians moving on to the mission, but also by protests from settlers who had been there first and resented the arrival of a crowd of 'goat-stealers'. However, gradually the mission settlement took shape. It was called the Joy Memorial Mission, as a Miss Joy and her sisters gave generously towards it in memory of their brother, an officer in the British army, who was killed in the First World War.

The Gospel was well received, and in November 1934, a year and a half after the missionaries arrived, the first eight converts were baptised, including Feliz Paz. Later a church was built under the direction of William Everitt, and evangelists started going out from San Patricio into the surrounding villages. (Several years later, Henry was visiting a group of Matacos contacted in this way, who lived about two hundred miles east of San Patricio on the railway line, when he was taken captive by the military for supposedly stirring up trouble between some nearby Tobas and the authorities. After an afternoon spent in a tiny cell which, he discovered, 'produces an echo and so enhances a singing voice', he was released and the matter was eventually sorted out.)

The evangelists also contacted other Matacos nearer San Patricio, at a place called Pozo Yacaré (the alligators' well), near the River Bermejo. The story of the birth of the mission at Pozo Yacaré has been beautifully told, if a bit idealised, in the SAMS magazine, under the title of 'Pericote's prayer':

The tropical sun beats down upon a sandy track winding its way through the dense, steaming tangle of forest and cactus. The air near the ground shimmers in the great heat, and all is still and silent in the forest, save for the occasional sharp hollow 'tap-tap' of the scarlet crested woodpecker exploring the bark of a shady tree. The wild life of the forest has sought sanctuary from the pitiless rays of the sun, all save the brightly coloured lizards, their green, red and purple bodies flashing in the sunlight as they dart here and there, resting now and then with throats pulsating, their long forked tongues flicking out with lightning speed at the unsuspecting fly or insect.

The approach of some travellers causes the lizards to scatter into the forest, and a company of Mataco Indians appears. They walk in single file, their sandals raising little clouds of dust at each step. One of the men is mounted upon a rather decrepit horse, he is Pericote, or Ama (Rat) – the chief of the Rat Indians, a small wizened man, whose body sways with the motion of the horse beneath him. The Indians have walked some thirty miles in the terrific heat that day, their destination the church service at San Patricio. For three years they have been asking for a missionary to be sent to their district, but lack of men and money has prevented the fulfilment of their request. At last they arrive and sit in the front rows on the sunbaked mud bricks which serve as seats. One phrase from the third collect for evening prayer catches the attention of Pericote, and he repeats it again and again: *'Hutune hap honatsi taj i-no-yejen opaltsen ame Thawuk'* (Lighten our darkness we beseech you, O Lord). Long after the last Indian has left the church and the sun has set, Pericote stays in the darkened church, praying in his heart to the great unknown chief in the skies: 'Lighten our darkness . . . Lighten our darkness . . .'

Ever since first hearing the Gospel from travelling evangelists from San Patricio, the people of Pozo Yacaré had been hoping for a mission, even migrating en bloc to San Patricio for a while, until local food supplies were hopelessly strained and they had had to go back home. The article goes on to tell how next day Pericote's prayer was answered, as it was decided that Walter Taylor, now at San Patricio, would leave the work there in the charge of his colleague Jack Gould for a while, and go with Pericote to start up a mission for his people. He described, also for the magazine, a service held at Pozo Yacaré a few months later:

The sun has set. Only the long-drawn hoots of an owl break the eerie stillness of the tropical night. The dark waters of the lagoon scintillate with the reflection from a hundred fires of the Indian villages surrounding it on all sides. At once the spell is broken by the strident notes of the mission 'bell'. (This latter is a length of discarded railway line, which upon being struck by a metal hammer gives forth a note not incomparable to that of Big Ben.)

The hitherto silent village comes to life. Men get up from resting on their animal skins, women cease spinning and weaving, dogs bark and fight fiercely together. Everybody makes for the missionary's house, a small mud building standing on the high bank of the lagoon. For today is '*Ifwalas Chowej*' (the days' middle) as Matacos call Wednesday; and the mid-week service is to be held. Very soon a crowd has collected, the people join reverently in prayer, and then pictures illustrating the life of Jesus are thrown on to a screen suspended between two trees. The beam of light from the carbide lantern attracts from the forest around moths, flying beetles and vampire bats innumerable; but the Indians' eyes are riveted on the magical screen, where they see for the first time the picture of our blessed Lord.

As he wrote, 'it was a great joy to see the first signs of the convicting and converting work of the Holy Spirit in the hearts of these primitive people, as one by one they gave expression in simple words to their longing to enter upon the

Christian life: 'I want to follow the Jesus trail' . . . 'It is good that I should learn God's words.''

In fact Walter Taylor had only been 'lent' to Pozo Yacaré from San Patricio, but at the end of August 1938 the people there welcomed their own resident missionaries with the arrival of William and Dorothy Everitt, complete with their parrot and two dogs.

William Everitt was a dedicated Christian and a craftsman. His wife, Dorothy, was the sister of Alfred Tompkins. They took over and built up the mission from scratch, first erecting the necessary houses, and then undertaking the various facets of the work between them. Their three children were born while they were there.

William was a very practical and a very generous man. Even before he came to the Chaco he gave most of the profits of his building trade to SAMS, and once there he was always working out schemes whereby the Indians could be taught useful trades. The chief of these was carpentry and furniture making, but at Pozo Yacaré the abundance of alligators in the lagoon led him to help the Indians in the selling of alligator skins. They were already hunting them, aware of a growing demand, and as Henry Grubb commented, 'We were quite pleased at this, for the alligator is an unpleasant reptile, very common in this part of the Chaco, and we felt that it would do no harm if its numbers were reduced.'

William undertook to collect the hides from the Indians and to get them to Los Blancos, fifty miles away by road. This involved not only the transport, but measuring, salting and packing them as well. Added to which the Indians liked to be paid in kind, so large quantities of goods had to be brought back from Los Blancos. As Henry commented again, 'Only a man of Mr Everitt's capabilities could have undertaken all this in addition to the other work of the mission.'

William worked out, too, a co-operative system within the mission – a kind of early version of the Welfare State – so that any profit was used to feed those unable to feed themselves, with rations for the elderly coming out of the central pool. A gentle and an energetic man, he would be up early in the mornings and working late into the night, his motto always to 'help the people'. Languages did not come easily to him, but he managed none-the-less to communicate extraordinarily well with the Indians, who loved him. Dorothy found languages easier, and concentrated on the medical work and later, of course, on bringing up their children.

The spiritual response at Pozo Yacaré was good, and soon there were conversions and baptisms, and the Indians themselves began helping with the services. And so throughout the 1930s the Gospel spread rapidly on the banks of the Bermejo as well as on the Pilcomayo.

15
Santa Maria

One more important development took place at this time – at Santa Maria on the Pilcomayo near the Bolivian border, the place where our story began. God's work at Santa Maria began with the wedding at Algarrobal, on July 6th, 1938, of two young English people: George Revill and Winifred Mellor. George had been brought up in the west of England in an 'open' Brethren family among whom missionary work was always a priority. Artistically inclined, when he left school he took the unusual job of window-display artist in a big store in London's West End. However, inspired by the life and early death of Fenton Hall, a missionary in the Amazon jungle, he soon felt the call himself to the unevangelised Indian tribes. He was studying at the Norwood missionary training colony and worshipping at St Paul's Church, Portman Square, when he first met Winifred Mellor.

Winnie and her elder sister Irene were enterprising girls who had recently come to London from Leeds, and were living in a hostel in Baker Street. Winnie, like George Revill, had an original mind. As she says, 'I could have had the chance of winning a scholarship to a university, but my father had no use for educated women. I'd have enjoyed the opportunity for learning more. Instead, I went to night-school and read almost every book in the local library.' She was secretary in a large printing firm. She had a flair for writing, too, and was writing the whole of the firm's house magazine under different names! This led to a short spell as a journalist, writing about new kitchens and labour-saving devices in connection with the building boom of the 1930s.

Winnie and Irene turned to Christ and dedicated their lives to him at St Paul's Church, Portman Square. A little later, out of loyalty to Irene, Winnie stood up with her at a meeting in response to a call for missionaries to China. Rightly, nothing came of this, and for a while Winnie responded to a call nearer at hand to spend her summer holiday taking the Gospel, with members of the Friends' Evangelistic Band (FEB), to people living on the new housing estates near Gravesend. A friend on the team was convinced that Winnie should be in full-time missionary work: 'I shall pray about it and ask the Lord for a sign,' said the friend.

'I shall want a very clear one,' said the reasonable Winnie.

'Then we'll pray for a soul through your ministry.'

Winifred continues the story:

'We were only there a week. One day as we went along, a little group of half a dozen people with a harmonium, we met a crowd of noisy children coming to meet us. So we prepared to hold our service and I was asked to speak. "Now's your chance, Lord," I said, and talked about the two processions of life and death, Jesus and his disciples meeting the widow of Nain. At the end I asked any little boy or girl who wanted to give his heart to Jesus to stay behind, and fourteen did. I thought there must be one in that lot, so I wrote to the FEB and told them what had happened.'

That was Winnie's sign. For a year she worked full time with the FEB, but soon felt dissatisfied:

'I remember with tears saying to the Lord, "Lord, there are churches at every street corner in England. What am I doing here?" My call, I felt, was to the unevangelised people of the world.'

After a year at Bible college, she hoped to go to Japan, but her uncertainties were resolved in an unexpected way.

'I had one of my rare bouts of illness – a slight attack of flu. Irene was now married, and I was staying with her. One morning she came in with a letter from George. I said, "Oh you read it!" I can see her face now as she said, "I think he's proposing to you!" I read it and replied, "I think he is!"'

'George and I were both thirty at the time and had become very good friends before he left; but there had been nothing romantic about it – our souls were above such things! He told me later that he had thought of proposing before, but he thought that he was meant to go to the Indians of Argentina, while I appeared to be heading for the other side of the world.

'I wrote back to George saying that I couldn't say yes or no until Japan had made up its mind. Eventually a letter came saying that the Society had decided to send no more missionaries to Japan, which was just as well as it was not long before Pearl Harbor. So we became officially engaged and I went out to join him.'

They were married by Mr Tompkins at Algarrobal, and as the SAMS magazine records, 'Six little Mataco girls, resplendent in white head-dresses, formed the choir, and sang in Mataco, "O perfect love" and "Praise, my soul, the King of heaven". Later in the day the bride and bridegroom left for their isolated home on the border between Bolivia and Argentina where they are witnessing to the Lord Jesus Christ chiefly to the Chiriguano Indians.'

In fact they were only here, still working for the Eastern Bolivian Mission, for a short time, while Mr and Mrs Dickson, the resident missionaries, were on furlough. They then set off for Santa Maria, the home of Mataco Indians on the northern stretches of the Pilcomayo in Argentina, where SAMS had not yet reached. Their adventures there were enchantingly described by Winifred, in her book *Chaco Chapters*[16]:

Her first sight of the Indians was the morning after their arrival, when

grouped around the doors and peering in at the cracks were Indian braves of far more lurid appearance than we had ever seen hanging around the bread shops and garbage-bins of the town. With long red or blue skirts, dangling earrings, faces shorn of eyebrows and eyelashes marked with blue pencil and red paint, they looked quite alarming. However they proved to be amiable, and with great gusto helped us to unload our lorry, in return for cupfuls of flour.

I think the lack of privacy was my greatest trial in those early days. It almost seemed as though the Indians had arranged among themselves never to leave us unattended. We ate, worked and sometimes took a midday siesta with our all too few apertures for air blocked by silent spectators.

Never had I seen such primitive dwellings as we found the Indians living in in Santa Maria. They were merely made of saplings formed into a beehive-shaped shelter with a small hole for a door. Outside each burned a fire, in most cases with a small smoke-blacked tin of vegetables or fish boiling on it. Packs of dogs, so thin that every bone showed through their skins, came rushing towards us with snarls and yaps, and for a few minutes the entire population was engaged in grabbing their dogs or throwing sticks at them.

At first we had no building in which to hold services or classes, so each afternoon my husband and I would settle ourselves on stools outside our house, and before long we would each have a large ring of scholars squatting on logs of wood. For slates at first they had only the sun-baked earth, and for pencils their forefingers.

It was after some months of this school-work that a tall silent Indian approached and handed them a slate on which was written in his own Mataco language, 'This man whose name is Ceja. I do not yet know my Lord God' – the beginning of understanding and response. Ceja was later converted and baptised.

Another man who later turned to Christ at Santa Maria was Carlos. A witch-doctor from San Luis, he heard the 'new' teaching on a visit to Santa Maria and moved there to live.

I didn't go to church, though [he remembered], I just sat and watched the people going to church, but I didn't know what they were doing. I was a coca-chewer and always had a big wad of it stuck in my cheek. One day I went to Pablo (the Revills' houseboy who had been converted and become an evangelist) and talked to him. He taught me a little and told me that coca and tobacco were bad things. So I gave up smoking and chewing coca and started going to school.

My head was hard, but slowly I learnt. Then suddenly it was as if I woke up: I understood God's words. I always tell people that if they really want to know God's words they can, but it does not happen quickly. God does answer our prayers.

Carlos himself became an evangelist and was later ordained and lived for many years at Pozo Tigré taking the Gospel to the people there.

Winifred described the countryside round Santa Maria: 'It is not a country of dense foliage and towering trunks. The soil is too poor for luxuriant growth. Small, gnarled trees with their twisted branches covered in beautiful grey-green lichen, bulging-trunked bottle-trees, weird clumps of cactus – these are the predominant features of the landscape that unfolds itself mile after mile as one journeys along its dusty roads.'

Winifred and George's two children, Ann and Michael, were born in Argentina, and George did wonders with the house, which had been built some years before as a store run by whites, but had been abandoned during the Bolivian-Paraguayan war. As the children grew up, Winifred commented that in spite of the dangers – snakes, eye infections, hook-worms, malaria, and even a small-pox epidemic with which George coped valiantly and with considerable skill

a house in an Indian village on the Pilcomayo is almost as good as a farm by the seaside. There are baby chicks to see, the excitement of collecting eggs, butterflies to chase, humming birds to watch busy about their nests around the house; fireflies twinkling in and out of the trees at bedtime; baby goats of confiding friendliness; pigs and piglets; donkeys and horses; wild berries to gather for the chickens;

walks in leafy country lanes; fine sand in little dunes and hollows on the river beach; and bathing.[16]

Of the Indians' way of life, she observed,

> Often when I go visiting, the Mataco mode of life seems a sunny carefree thing. There they sit, under a rustic shade outside their huts, doing their little tasks and eating their simple food, with brown babies tumbling about in the sunshine and domestic fowls coming for a drink. But when I go sick-visiting, their lot does not seem to be so happy. The patient lies inside the hut, usually on the floor, with draughts blowing through the straw walls and smoke drifting across the hut. Sickness to them is not only a pain or disorder, it is a fearsome thing.

She goes on to describe the fear associated with illness and death – in particular the fear that when a child dies, the released spirit is angry at having to leave the body so soon, and that it returns to haunt its former home.

> They remind one of children in so many ways. Like children, they live for the moment. Like children, too, they take for granted any care that is bestowed upon them, and in their fears of the unknown they are very like children, crying in the dark.

16
Ups and Downs

In the late 'thirties and early 'forties various changes took place in the Argentine Chaco. Alfred Leake went to England in 1938 to spend a year studying for ordination. The Toba mission meanwhile was run by Alfred and Dora Tebboth, who had married in Buenos Aires in 1938. Dora, who had met 'Teb' at his home church in Croydon, wrote regular letters home which give a vivid picture of their life at that time. For example, 'An old Toba had sore eyes, so we put drops in them and gave him a little lotion in a sterile bottle. Some days later he complained that the medicine wasn't any good because he had tried it on his aching foot and it wasn't any better!'

Soon after Easter, a mighty exodus took place, the Tobas – men, women and children – walking the fifty miles to the railway station at Juarez for their work at the cane-fields. Dora wrote, 'Hundreds will be away until November. I hope those Christians who have gone will keep straight, for it is awful to hear some of the things these Indians get up to at the cane-fields.'

Sure enough, they were back in November, and Dora wrote, 'You should have seen the new trousers, bombachas, skirts, shirts, coats, vests, shoes, socks, hats, caps, boaters, handkerchiefs, cheap rings, balls, soap, cigarettes, food and goodness knows what else, ducks, horses and dogs!'

In fact the annual exodus to the cane-fields, which kept many whole Indian families away from their villages for eight or nine months of the year, was of doubtful benefit in many ways. On the one hand it meant that the communities in which missionaries were based were considerably depleted for much of the time; and the Indians themselves seemed to lose almost as much as they gained by these trips. The work

was hard, and both illness and immorality were rife. Sometimes children would be left alone all day on the encampment
while mother and father, taking babies with them, went to
work.

Despite the cheerfulness of the workaday scene, at night
drunkenness, gambling and the chants of the witch-doctors
were evidence of the potent influence of 'town civilisation' on
the one hand and paganism on the other. In such a setting
only the truly converted, strong Christian would stand.

Year by year, faithful evangelists would go with their
people to the cane-fields and, in the face of the mockery of
unbelievers, call them together for the ministry of God's
word. And at the end of it all the gullible Indian would be
readily exploited by storekeepers or by the lorry driver who
gave him a lift home, so that much of his hard-earned gains
would evaporate almost at once.

Dora delighted, too, in observing the brilliantly coloured
varieties of birds in the area, the butterflies and flowers. As
well as supporting 'Teb' energetically in his work (she helped
with dispensing the medicines, and in particular ran groups
for the children so that their mothers could partake in
the church services undisturbed), she had a keen eye for
everything beautiful, as this description shows.

I do miss the twilight. Yesterday at sunset I noticed the sky
– it was absolutely glorious in the west, not streaked with
colour, but a flood of the most wonderful ripe strawberry
colour I ever saw, with a dash of polished copper added.
You know how the sun looks on a frosty day – a ball of red –
all the sky was like that. It reflected in the blue sky of the
east, and as daylight faded the east was a pale greyish
heliotrope and in it was the brass face of the full moon
which was quite bright although the sun had not set. Teb
and I walked to the main gate and in this wonderful
half-light we saw in the distance a long, long stretch of mist
hovering between earth and the tree-tops, for between us
and the trees is a wide open space, part of which is a
football pitch.

Voices were heard singing a familiar hymn tune to Toba
words issuing from a prayer-hut some little way off, and
with the leap of a fire outside a silhouetted hut, the bray of
a donkey, the voices of the Indians in conversation, and the
last twitter and flutter of a bird before it settled down, a
perfect picture was there, a coloured sound-picture which
is now lost except to my memory. We returned to the
house, to a small fire, slippers, letters and wireless; truly a
comfortable evening.

It was at about this time that the second Toba mission,
Mision Pilaga, had to be abandoned. This was partly because of the drying up of the lagoon, but other troubles had
contributed as well. Alfred Tebboth has written an account
of the disastrous massacre of Tobas from Mision Pilaga
which occurred at Campo Quemado in 1937. Before his
marriage he had been seconded there from MET to replace
first John Arnott and then Bill Price who were going home on
leave.

My fellow missionary, Bill Price, spent much time out
hunting in the forest with the Indians. On one occasion he
went with a party of them to their old district which had
been taken over by the Argentinian gendarmerie in order
to secure the frontier and was therefore forbidden territory
for the Indian tribes. It was there that he met the captain
in charge of the fort and detachment. This officer and his
Irish wife were glad to meet an Englishman, and Bill
invited them to visit Mision Pilaga some time.

Unfortunately by the time this invitation was taken up,
Bill had left for England and I was the only missionary
there. When they arrived unannounced at Mision Pilaga,
consternation was general and great at the sight of military
uniform, but those Indians who had been on the hunting
trip previously with Bill Price were pleased to recognise
the army captain. They immediately set about obtaining
permission to hunt ostriches near the fort. But there was no
Bill Price to go with them on this trip!

The captain said he would allow them to hunt in his area

provided they had a note from me saying that they were mission Indians and not some of the wilder variety. The Indians were very pleased at this. They made preparations by way of obtaining cartridges for their shotguns and making provision for their stay for a few days away from home while they shot ostriches in order to obtain their saleable feathers etc. When they left they carried a note from me saying that they were nine mission Indians of good behaviour and that any complaints should be notified to me. This 'passport' would have been one of their most guarded possessions.

Some days later, I had finished taking school one morning when I heard the death-chant coming from huts in the village. I thought little of it at the time because it was a common occurrence for a widow on a dull day to recall the death of her late husband and to mourn him in the death-wail. However I soon learnt that one of the huntsmen had arrived back in the village. He told a sad tale. The group had been taken prisoner by the 'palefaces' and shot dead. He had managed to escape and come back with the news.

Knowing the propensity of the Indians to romance (their dream-life is as real to them as their waking existence), I rather underplayed the matter until the arrival of another man who had escaped confirmed the story. Then I knew I must do something about it. With a trusted Indian guide I rode overnight to the fort. We found that the reports were all too true – seven Indians had been shot dead. The captain said that he himself had only just returned from a visit to Buenos Aires and had not been in command of the fort when the Indians had arrived. Apparently they had approached a local Spanish storekeeper and asked for some sugar and yerba maté on account – to be paid for in ostrich feathers after the hunt. The storeman had become frightened. Thinking they were savage Indians he had sent to the fort for help. A sergeant and other soldiers had arrived, tied the Indians' hands behind their backs in one room and sent them into the next room, at each corner of which was stationed a soldier.

They opened fire and killed seven of the nine would-be hunters. Only two had escaped.

Being unable to obtain any satisfaction or apology we returned to the mission. We found the men assembled and ready to go on the warpath, a thing they had not done for years. It would have meant wholesale slaughter. I managed to persuade them not to take revenge but to stay quietly in their huts. Meanwhile I sent for Alfred Leake at Mision El Toba because his knowledge of the Indians and their ways was much greater than my own. He advised them in the same strain as I had imperfectly done. Together he and I concocted letters which we addressed to the governor of the territory of Formosa and the colonel in charge of the garrison in this northern area, and other influential Argentinian authorities. We awaited eagerly the replies which we felt sure would at least inform us that the incident was to be investigated and dealt with in order to allay the fears and unrest of the Indians.

Weeks passed. Then one Saturday evening as I was preparing for my Sunday duties an Indian arrived with a telegram. This had followed the usual course in these out-of-the-way places of being passed to the local store and thence into the hands of a reliable person who was going in the right direction. It was from the Colonel in charge of the military zone and said that he would be arriving by train at Juarez early on Sunday morning, and he wished to meet me there to discuss the matter. Juarez was seventy-five miles away. It was impossible to catch a horse in the dark so with an Indian companion I walked all night through the dark and eerie forest to Mision El Toba. Arriving in the early hours of Sunday morning there was no time for sleep, but I managed to persuade the storekeeper at Sombrero Negro to take me the remaining fifty miles to Juarez in his lorry.

Imagine my dismay when upon arrival and enquiry at the local hotel I found that the Colonel who had made the assignation had not come on the train and had sent no apology or explanation. Neither did we hear any more from him or from the other people in authority to whom we had written. Back we had to go to face the expectant Indians. You can imagine the reaction of these simple people at this anticlimax. Inevitably a loss of confidence in the power and authority of the missionaries was brought about. Combined with the drying up of the water in the lagoon on which Mision Pilaga was situated, and the shortage of missionaries due to the war, the ultimate result was the scattering of the Indians to other parts of the Toba area and the closing of the mission station of Mision Pilaga.

The closing of Mision Pilaga was a setback. And in 1939 several of the younger missionaries left, some in response to the outbreak of war, some for other reasons. The Panter family left El Yuto as we have seen – temporarily at first, for health reasons; but because of the war they could not return, and settled down to a fruitful ministry in Gloucestershire.

Another disappointment to the missionaries was the decision of the Argentine government to take over the school at Algarrobal. 'The Indians do not want it,' Henry Grubb observed in his diary, but it took place none-the-less in November 1940. It became a government school, with all the lessons being taught in Spanish, and in fact as Bishop David Leake points out, the policy of the government in assuming responsibility for the educational and eventually the medical work was correct.

Henry had hoped to get back to England on his mother's death in 1939, but was prevented by the outbreak of war. By 1940 the missionary team in Argentina was considerably depleted. However, they managed between them to run the main stations of Mision Chaqueña, San Andres, Mision el Toba, San Patricio and Pozo Yacaré, and received a bonus when in 1943 the Revills at Santa Maria felt that the only way forward for them was to resign from the Eastern Bolivian Mission which was in financial difficulties and to link up with SAMS. Thus, as Henry put it, 'Santa Maria, a mission in full running order, became part of our field.'

Harry Dickson, who also, with his wife, joined SAMS from the Eastern Bolivian Mission, has described the change at

Santa Maria during the time the Revills were there: when he
first arrived there one midnight in 1938 to help George Revill
to repair the disused store which was to be the Revills' first
home,

> we found the Indians in the midst of a drunken brawl.
> Daylight revealed a wild-looking crowd of painted
> drunken folk in all stages of undress . . . the witch-doctor
> adopted a menacing attitude. Three years later, what a
> change I saw: by the faithful preaching of the Gospel and
> by much patience and kindness, opposition was elimin-
> ated. Every service was crowded with friendly men,
> women and children all anxious to learn these new words.
> To listen to the singing was a thrilling experience, and how
> they listened to the address!

The mission of Santa Maria can be seen as a focal point in the
design of God's weaving, the story of his work in the Argentine Chaco. Near here, many years earlier, the Franciscans
on retiring from their work had prayed earnestly for God's
light to shine once more on the people they had loved and
sought to serve and bring to Christ; here, some thirty or forty
years after the Revills' arrival, Helena Oliver, the well-
to-do Argentinian brought up in the same Roman Catholic
faith as the Franciscans who had prayed, was to be brought
to a deeper and full commitment by the Indians for whom
they had prayed.

In fact the Revills did not stay at Santa Maria very long
after joining up with SAMS. Encroachment of the banks of
the river due to severe flooding in 1944 led to the decision to
move some thirty miles downstream – i.e. nearer to San
Andres – to the site of a mixed Mataco and Choroti village
known as La Paz. George managed, against heavy odds, to
build a new house for them there, and Winifred and the
two children eventually moved, George showing his usual
ingenuity in bringing a final load downstream on a home-
made raft.

Most of the Indians at the now flourishing mission and
church at Santa Maria decided to stay where they were – a

decision which was vindicated as the rich supply of fish in the river led to trade with the nearby towns developing there. The church was left in the charge of Pablo, who had been the Revills' houseboy and was, as Winifred recorded, 'quite the most outstanding Indian character we have come across'.

The Christians at Santa Maria, supported by visits from the Revills from La Paz, continued to run the school, the church services, Sunday school and women's meeting. They were also invited to preach to a small group of Matacos living thirty miles to the north, at Crevo, across the Bolivian border – a village which had been named after the French explorer, Jules Crévaux, who had been murdered there so many years before – and here an enthusiastic church began to grow.

Sadly though, it has to be said that later the church in Santa Maria went temporarily through a very low time, so that a missionary visiting in the 1960s was struck both by the dirty and uncared-for appearance of the village and by the low spiritual state of the church. Pablo and many others had turned back to their old ways, and the church itself had abandoned its prayer-meetings and only met once on a Sunday – the evening service having also been abandoned so that the men were free to fish in readiness for the fish lorries which made their collections at the weekends.

The new mission at La Paz prospered. It was a complex situation, as the Indians there had a bad reputation for stealing goats from their Spanish-speaking neighbours, and they included among their number murderers, drunkards, coca-leaf addicts and dealers in contraband. As elsewhere, babies were sometimes killed by their mothers at birth, especially if crippled or one of a pair of twins.

In addition, the Matacos who lived there were soon joined by Chorotis and Chunupis from across the river, all three tribes speaking different languages. The Chorotis were a small tribe of short, laughing people who had never heard the Gospel. With the aid of interpreters the Revills translated a few portions of Scripture and one or two hymns and choruses for them. For the Chunupis, a larger and wilder tribe, they were able at that stage to do little.

In 1950 George and Winifred Revill left for England, and their place at La Paz was taken by Harry Dickson and his wife, Maisie. Harry, a sorting clerk with the Post Office in Newcastle, had been converted at the age of 17 through a remarkable set of circumstances leading him to attend the Keswick Convention. He and Maisie both felt called to work in South America and, like the Revills, they went initially to work with the Eastern Bolivian Mission. Their work was among the Chiriguano Indians both at the cane-fields at La Esperanza and also at San Antonio, where John Linton had worked on the Parapiti River.

In 1943, together with the Revills, they left the Eastern Bolivian Mission and joined SAMS, but whereas the Revills stayed at Santa Maria where they had already begun to work, the Dicksons went for a while to Algarrobal to learn Mataco, then to help Henry Grubb at San Andres, and then for five very fruitful years to Pozo Yacaré. There they took over the work of the Everitts, who had gone to set up an important carpentry industry at Algarrobal. The Dicksons were at Pozo Yacaré between about 1946 and 1950, and during their time they witnessed a remarkable revival there. The enthusiasm of the early days had worn off, and the spiritual life there seemed at a low level, with several instances of immorality among church members, when, as Henry Grubb has described,

an Indian from another area, who had recently been in contact with a pentecostal group, came on a visit to the mission. He began to tell the Indians about his new life, and immediately it was as if he had set a match to a heap of dry tinder. True at first there were excesses, and an emphasis on the subjective side of the faith, but these were transitory. Not only was there new life in the services, but many of the Christians began to show an interest in the spiritual welfare of their neighbours, white and Indian, and started to hold services for their white neighbours, a thing which had never happened before.

Many small Christian communities around the River Bermejo owe their beginnings to the church at Pozo Yacaré: for example in 1946 faithful evangelists made the three-day journey by foot to a small village called Saucelito, just south of the river. Not only did they preach the Gospel, but they taught the people to read, so that soon this small church had among its members some who could read the Bible for themselves.

Also, south of the river is a beautiful village, Laguna Sauzal, its houses scattered round the edges of a peaceful lagoon frequented by many species of water-bird. The Christians here also first heard the good news of Jesus Christ in 1946 from a Pozo Yacaré evangelist who was working with them in the cotton-fields in Formosa province. When their work was finished they made the long trek to Pozo Yacaré in order to learn more, and then the chief (one of the first to be converted) and the small group of Christians went back home to found their own church at Laguna Sauzal.

In the little village of Campo Tres Pozos, too, are Christians grateful for the fact that 'in the past when no one else had pity on us, the Anglicans did!' William Everitt, 'a man who knew our words', William White, and an evangelist from Pozo Yacaré had all helped them, and they were grateful. It was difficult though at times to maintain consistent Bible teaching in all these churches, and without that they cannot grow.

As well as reaching out to other Indian communities, the church at Pozo Yacaré has succeeded in a task that the social situation and their own diffidence usually render too daunting to the Indians – that of sharing the Christian message with their *Criollo* (Argentinian settler) neighbours. One or two Spanish-speaking families have been converted through Indian Christians; some Indians working in Embarcacion or in the saw-mills of Juarez will hold services in Spanish as well as in Mataco for the benefit of their Spanish-speaking neighbours, and on Christmas day a fiesta is held at Pozo Yacaré, with sports and a service in Spanish in the evening, to which many settler families come, all dressed in their best, and hear testimonies from the Indian believers.

At Pozo Yacaré, too, the Dicksons met an Indian boy who later was to become a key figure in the church in Argentina, Mario Mariño. His father, a hunter, having been attracted by William Everitt's trade in alligator skins had brought his wife and children to Pozo Yacaré from Saucelito. Now their mother brought her two sons to the school. In poor health herself, she doted on her boys and wanted the very best for them. They were both very intelligent and Mario later became a pupil-teacher. Rosa, a bright girl who helped Maisie in the kitchen, was later to become Mario's wife. Later, Mario and his brother Ernesto were both ordained, Mario becoming eventually the first Indian bishop of the diocese of Northern Argentina, and Ernesto becoming the pastor of the flourishing church of Saucelito.

Mario remembers both the Everitts and the Dicksons at Pozo Yacaré as follows:

> William Everitt was a great man of valour in many ways. To this day we do not know how a man had so much to do and yet completed his work. Mrs Everitt was also a very active person who received people into her home, talking with them all the time. I learnt a lot from both of them. Henry Dickson was a great preacher and teacher – he enjoyed singing, too. He was very friendly and understood our language very well. He enjoyed fishing and shooting and football – he wanted to do all the things the people did. The Dicksons asked me to teach in the Sunday school, and I learnt much from them about pastoral counselling too. They treated me almost like a son, and used to ask me about my future. I would reply, 'I'm a man now, and I should work. But I promise I'll do something for the Lord.'

In 1950, with the church at Pozo Yacaré strong and able, generally, to be run by Indian leaders supported by visiting missionaries, the Dicksons were free to move to La Paz, many miles north on the Pilcomayo, to take over the work there from the Revills. Here, too, the faithful preaching and patient work of both couples bore remarkable fruit, and many of the former murderers and coca-leaf addicts were converted, as was old Alfredo Gonzalez, a noted witch-doctor. He and his wife set up a Christian home, and their two older sons, David and Lucas, of whom more later, became two of the most valued helpers on the mission. Goat-stealing from the settlers became a rare event.

It was in 1950 that God began also to work among the Chunupis, the large tribe from across the river. While they were away at the cane-fields, an epidemic broke out among them and they became very ill and frightened. Although the Matacos and Chunupis were enemies, it was Pablo, the Mataco evangelist from Santa Maria, who came to help them.

'Our God who is in heaven can save us from our sins,' he told them. 'He can also heal. When we are sick, we pray to the Lord and he hears and helps us. He can heal us, but if not, we know we are going to heaven. Now bring your sick people here and lay them on the ground.'

Pablo then prayed: 'Lord, you can do anything. Here our Chunupi friends are sick and many have died already. We pray that you will heal these sick people.' God heard the prayer, and every one of the sick who were prayed for that day recovered.

Soon afterwards, some Matacos came running to Harry Dickson at La Paz: 'Henrique, come quickly! The Chunupis are crossing the river.' They were coming, about two hundred of these wild-looking Indians, with all their goods and chattels. They wanted to settle at the mission and learn God's word. Harry, with help from bilingual Indians, set about meeting this need, and so the Gospel spread to the Chunupis.

The work at La Paz was not easy, and it was a tribute to the power of the Gospel that three tribes could live together in one village at all. Frequently each part of a service had to be repeated in each of three languages. Frequently the hot north wind blew up so much dust that the river was invisible for days on end. But the Christians, both missionary and Indian, persevered, and God honoured them.

Mataco man mending fishing net.

17
Ripe for Change

The Leake family, with three children now, David, Cristina and Dorothy, were at Mision El Toba all this time, persevering patiently with the ups and downs of the turbulent Tobas. Alfred, as we shall see, had often to be away, visiting the many small churches and outstations, preaching and administering the sacraments there.

His wife Dorothy kept a happy and stable home going for the children, and managed to do much work among the Indian women and children herself. She taught in the school, went visiting, and in particular encouraged the women to improve and increase their weaving and string-bag work so that the things they made could be sold in the cities. Gradually a small business was built up. Dorothy herself had had dressmaking training and made most of her children's clothes herself on her sewing-machine. In addition, she saw to her own children's education when they were small.

They had a comfortable and spacious house which Alfred, helped by the Tobas, had built of sun-baked bricks with a corrugated iron roof and an earth floor. As the younger Dorothy has said,

> My father was very practical – he seemed to be able to turn his hand to anything. We didn't have much furniture or possessions, but even so I often felt conscious that we had so much more than the Indians had. We had hot and cold running water and elementary plumbing, and rustic but good furniture. My father, I remember, once gave my mother a settee which he had designed and our Toba carpenter made, as a birthday present.

Their childhood was wonderfully happy and free. Little Dorothy, several years younger than the other two, depended entirely on Indian children for playmates when David and

Cristina were away at school. They used to make little 'dolls'
– figures of clay – and build themselves small houses like the
Indians' huts. She identified completely with them, and
loved them dearly.

David, too, felt that he was richly privileged in his upbringing, with its tremendous sense of freedom – riding,
hunting, freedom to wander where one liked. As he says now,
one would have to be a privileged person indeed to enjoy
these things in England, and to own five horses, as he did. He
would go into the *monte* shooting and hunting with the Indian
boys and became, like them, well versed in reading the
footprints and other forest marks. The Indians were very
skilled in interpreting such signs: animal droppings and
tracks, surface disturbances of the river, the buzzing of a bee
in flight would indicate not only the presence of food but also
what sort of food it might be. David became adept at rod- and
spear-fishing, too, but unlike the Indian children the Leakes
made sure they kept out of the river when the piranha fish,
which could take a big bite out of one's leg, were around.

Travelling was exciting, too, and David loved to go upriver
in the cart or as outrider with his father. Despite the fact that
he was sent to boarding-school in Buenos Aires from the age
of 8, going in early March and not coming home again until
November, David was always conscious of a great sense of
security and permanence in his childhood – both in his home
and within the Indian village community.

At home Alfred and Dorothy always set aside Monday
evening for the family to play games and be together; every
day, too, they had family prayers. Saturday was a great day,
with the upstream Indians all congregating, camping round
the fires, ready for the service the next day. And on Sunday
afternoon, when the visitors had saddled up and set off home,
Alfred and Dorothy would go visiting round the village and
the children, dressed in white (their Sunday best), with little
white hats, would go too. As David remembers,

My parents had a big stick, to keep the dogs away. We'd
start at the point in the village where we'd left off the
previous week and keep going till it was time for evening

prayer at six. Then they'd go back and ring the bell for evening service and next Sunday we'd start again where we left off. It was a visit, but it also had something of the nature of an inspection – if things weren't clean enough, the family would be told to sweep up!

And of his school, St Alban's in Buenos Aires, David remembers,

It was a school founded very much on British public-school principles – discipline, sport, Rugby and so on. We spoke Spanish in the mornings and English in the afternoons, a rule which was strictly enforced. Here I met the children of wealthy British businessmen and equally wealthy Argentines. I enjoyed the two totally different worlds of school and home and made many good friends in both. Living in these two worlds enabled me to be at home in the languages and ways of the Tobas, the Matacos, the English and the Argentines. Thus I developed naturally the gift of communicating with all these different people which is so valuable today.

Interestingly, one of David's contemporaries at St Alban's was Luis Palau, the evangelist, who in his autobiography remembers him like this: 'Leake didn't flaunt his faith. He was just faithful, steady. He never talked piously. He was just himself, and he was admired and respected.'

Another of David's school friends was Victor Everitt, son of William and Dorothy. The Everitts were by now at Algarrobal, where William was establishing a furniture-making business which proved to be one of the most enduring and valuable practical developments of the mission. It was centred at Algarrobal – 'the gateway to the Indian villages' – a good spot, as not only was it near the railway, but a good supply of cedarwood was available, being brought down in the floods from higher up in the Andes. Victor remembers what happened next:

The Indians pulled the logs in to the side and the next thing was to cut them up. We had big saw-pits and men would spend days, one on top of the log and one underneath, just cutting. Then when the wood had been seasoned it was used for making furniture to my father's designs. Timber for special orders was cut from the forest – lignum-vitae, which in England would be a very expensive wood. Dad used to get orders from as far as Buenos Aires – we made chairs for some schools there. It was mostly fairly rustic furniture, all made by hand, and gradually the Indians learnt to do it all themselves.

The patterns established by William Everitt are still in use today. He did many other things as well – designing and building some of the mission churches, as we have seen; digging wells; making shot for guns; as well as working as the wheelwright and blacksmith for the mission.

As far as missionary personnel were concerned, things were getting harder. Some had left at the outbreak of war, and more left when it ended. Some of these had had long spells without a break because of the war. Henry Grubb, with typical self-effacement and generosity, allowed his fellow missionaries the opportunity of going home before leaving himself, and it wasn't until 1949 that he eventually went back to Britain after fourteen years away without a break.

There he married Olive Leake who had left Argentina many years earlier to look after her elderly parents in East Runton, and who now returned with him to the work. It was said that he had been alone so much that at one mission station he had taken to sitting at a different side of the supper table each day as a way of introducing variety!

Although based at Algarrobal as mission superintendent, he had frequently had spells at the other village missions, running them, often single-handed, as need arose. Alfred Tompkins and his wife resigned from the mission in 1945, and the Tebboths left in 1947. Dora Tebboth with her lively mind had observed many things during her time spent among the Tobas.

For example: 'The Indians' jump from nothing to civilis-ation in one hop is too much for them. This is one result of their going to the cane-fields. Then they declare that they are cheated and exploited, which is true; because they are not capable of dealing with a white man's modern world.' But that they were deliberately exploited and oppressed cannot be denied. The missionaries increasingly saw one of their roles as supporting them and enabling them to cope.

Sadly, during the 1940s, backsliding was widespread among the Chaco Christians. It showed itself in various ways: in recurrences of the dancing with its attendant immorality; in a resurgence of faith in witch-doctoring, and in addiction to coca. At Mision El Toba, one of the most difficult characters was an Indian known as Caradura (Hard-face), who had been an inveterate thief and coca-addict for many years. He would steal from the mission and the Indians' gardens in order to have something to offer to the settlers in exchange for coca-leaves. His addiction, and that of many other Indians, was learnt from and encouraged by the settlers. Indeed, according to Alfred Leake, even the policeman who had come to arrange for Caradura's arrest, when invited to come in for some coffee, replied, 'No thank you, sir, I'm going to take a little coca.'

This was a worrying problem, and there were others. With the encroachment of civilisation, food seemed harder to obtain by the old hunting and gathering methods, and yet the Indians – even the Christians – found it hard to make the cultural change to wage-earning. They did work at their gardens, but not only was the climate often against them but the settlers' cattle would often break in and wreak havoc among the crops.

Their life was less straightforward than it used to be, in many ways. Henry Grubb observed the following changes:

The gradual disappearance of native dress; the use of Spanish in all official dealings – more and more Indians becoming conversant with it; schools taken over by the government; the old nomadic way of life giving way to settled villages and wage-earning for a living. Nothing we can do will in the long run stem the process, even granted that to do so were desirable; we can only prepare the Indian so that he may not be thrown off his feet by it.

However, these outward changes don't always involve a corresponding change in mental or spiritual outlook. Thus an Indian may come to us for medicines and yet still believe he has a goat in his chest, a deer in his nose, or a beetle wandering round his anatomy. Equally, although he earns more than he used, he has no idea how to use the extra money to improve his standard of living . . .[17]

Another curious development which began in the early 1940s looked deceptively like a wonderful work of God. Starting with the evangelistic efforts of an American missionary couple who worked among the southern Tobas from a base at Resistencia some two hundred miles from MET, it appeared that thousands of Toba Indians were responding to the good news of Jesus Christ. The movement or cult was described in a paper by Elmer S. Miller, of Temple University, as a 'syncretism of traditional views on health, disease, spirits, witchcraft, and general cosmology with modern Pentecostal emphases on faith healing, glossolalia, and other forms of spirit possession.'[18] He observed that the movement occurred on the heels of the disintegration of traditional subsistence practices and authority structures, when confidence in traditional leadership had been seriously shaken by the inability of the shamans to treat the new diseases introduced by the settlers. It seemed that 'once the Toba will to retain the old ceremonial had gone, there was a vacuum which pentecostal Christianity was ideally suited to fill.' This could have been good, had the teaching been understood.

Healings, the incorporation of dancing and enthusiastic singing, and lengthy emotional services drew the Indians in, but sadly there was little Biblical teaching – at least little that was grasped. The Americans made the serious mistake of teaching in Spanish rather than in Toba, with the result that the Bible was regarded with superstitious honour, but its teaching was neither absorbed nor put into practice. Similarly the lengthy prayers consisted largely of ecstatic utterances mixed with smatterings of Spanish.

Despite its widespread appeal, this cult did little, because of its inadequate teaching, to build up the Christian church in the Chaco. It spread, however, to the Matacos, and the drums of these *Zapallos* (pumpkins – named after one of their leaders) are often nowadays still heard at night, along with the dancing, the endlessly repeated Spanish choruses and the 'spitting out of sin'. Meanwhile, the missionaries watched and prayed, and tried to use the lean war years to consolidate their work, and to strengthen the Indians to cope, in Christ, within the strong but flexible structure of the Anglican church.

In 1944 the missions themselves faced a crisis when Henry Grubb, as superintendent, was served with an order from the chief of police of the province of Formosa demanding the immediate cessation of all Protestant teaching of the Indians, to accord with the constitution of the Argentine Republic which states that native peoples must be taught Roman Catholicism. Apparently the order was the result of a complaint, but as Dora Tebboth pointed out, 'the fruits of our labours are hundreds of rational beings, literate and Christian.' After a moving meeting, with the Indians as disappointed and sad as the missionaries, all church and school work was closed down on the mission stations, only the medical work being allowed to continue. In the following year the Governor of the Territory of Formosa and the Chief of Police from whom the order had come resigned, and gradually the mission work started up again.

Life in Argentina as a whole was changing too. Juan Perón with his powerful wife Eva came to power in 1946. Despite their often dubious tactics, the next six years until Eva's untimely death saw the most positive achievements of the Perón regime: bringing the railways into Argentine hands, nationalising other public services, establishing a national airline and a merchant fleet, initiating labour legislation and an income distribution policy, building hospitals and schools and establishing industries – the construction, in fact, of modern Argentina.

Perón made a big show of identifying with the *descamisados* (the shirtless ones) – the workers – and attempted to improve their lot, while Eva, through the Eva Perón Foundation, supported various altruistic schemes in a munificent but haphazard and highly unconstitutional way. Most of these changes took a long time to affect the Chaco Indians. They were hundreds of miles from Buenos Aires, where the action was. Nonetheless, they *were* affected, and many Indians became 'politically aware' for the first time as they realised that here was a leader who cared about the welfare of the poor. Even now many thinking Indians vote for the Peronist party for this reason. Initially the Roman Catholic church supported Perón, but later on his high-handed methods, which had always infuriated the land-owning upper classes, began to alienate the church leaders as well. In 1955 he was overthrown in a right-wing military coup and spent almost twenty years in exile in Spain, to be brought back for a final year as President as the only man with any hope of uniting the country, shortly before he died in 1974.

The Tebboths left at the beginning of 1947, exhausted after nearly ten years, and 'Tomás' was eventually ordained in the Church of England. No replacements for the missionaries who had left were immediately forthcoming, and the early fifties were a very lean time, with a small band of missionaries trying to supervise a considerably expanded field. For example, La Paz alone was surrounded by many outstations, where small churches had been set up as a result of visits by Indian evangelists and missionaries, and where church services and a school were now run by an evangelist. To give extra teaching to these men who were taking responsibility for teaching others, evangelists' weeks were instituted at La Paz, and they used to walk ten to twenty miles in order to benefit from the fellowship and teaching of that week.

One difficulty for the Pilcomayo churches at this time was that once Alfred Tompkins and William White left, Alfred Leake, who had been ordained in 1938, was the only ordained man there. The small congregations, scattered over hundreds of miles, depended solely on him for the administration of the sacraments, which meant that baptisms and Holy Communion could only take place when he was able to visit. Many times he did the journey up the Pilcomayo from MET to Santa Maria and back – about three hundred miles the round trip, visiting all the churches in turn. Mercifully they were well spaced out and often he would reach the next church conveniently at the end of a day.

But it wasn't easy. The Chaco is a difficult place to travel in for much of the year. In the hot season it can be a sea of mud and water, while in the cooler, dry season many parts are ankle deep or more in dust. In the early days these journeys had been undertaken on horseback or occasionally by cart; later Alfred had acquired an old 1928 model A Ford which he bought for £80 – providentially just the amount he had saved up from gifts from the Missionary Association of his home village of East Runton.

It was fortunate that his spell of garage work as a boy had given him the knowledge he needed for repairs, though as the car grew older Alfred found himself spending more time tinkering with the works than actually driving. Once when he was miles from anywhere an axle broke, and it was eight days before he was able to get back to the stranded car with a replacement. Once, too, in 1941, he did a trip of 1737 miles by train, river-launch, cart and on horseback to take communion to all the Christian settlements in the Paraguayan Chaco which at that time had no ordained minister.

When he arrived at a village there was great excitement, and it could be many hours before he could settle down to rest. A crowd would quickly gather and sit round the fire, asking for news of the other villages and relating happenings in their own. Gradually they would drift away as the night drew on, but there would still often be some who were hoping for a private talk. Some might have fallen into sin; ought they to come to the Lord's table? Others had different problems, and the task of getting to know couples in the different churches at all before baptising their babies proved extremely difficult, so that for a while the practice of infant baptism was dropped altogether.

Alfred found it hard to keep giving of his best spiritually, and yet often the Indians had been waiting for months for his

visit. In fact the Rev. William Underwood and his wife joined
the mission in 1946, but they were based at San Patricio and
their work did not extend to the Pilcomayo. One missionary,
Bertie Harland, became ordained especially to meet this
need, but then illness forced him and his wife to leave South
America in 1960. By 1957 two more ordained people had
joined the mission – Francis Tompkins, son of Alfred Tompkins, and the Rev. John Bradberry and his wife – and so
Alfred, whose family had left the Chaco in 1954 because of
the children's educational needs, resigned too and took up a
living in Norfolk.

He had pioneered and served the growing churches in the
Argentine Chaco for thirty years. He had watched primitive
peoples, steeped in the fears and superstitions of countless
generations, come into the liberating power and peace of the
Gospel. Because the spirit world had been so real to them, it
had not been impossibly difficult for them to come to believe
in the supreme Good Spirit, and to expect to see him at work.
Their simple prayers had been very real and specific, as
during the war when one of them had prayed that Hitler's
guns would rust and his gunpowder get wet. Thus the church
which had grown up, despite its many shortcomings, was a
praying church, with a real concern for others in need and for
its own fellows who were still living in paganism.

This church had produced able preachers and evangelists,
and the Indians themselves had erected simple church buildings in many villages. Alfred himself became certain that the
next step forward was the ordination of several of the older
tried and trusted Christians, but for many years nothing
was done because of their lack of academic qualifications. Alfred was asked if he could recommend a younger
up-and-coming Indian Christian for ordination, but he felt
that in a culture where age and experience counts for much,
this would be wrong. And so for some years nothing was
done. The church in the Chaco was struggling, and ripe for
change.

18
A New Approach

A new missionary went out to the Argentine Chaco in 1955 –
Barbara Kitchen. Daughter of a railway worker, she had
developed a taste for travel young, when at the age of 8 or 9
she used to spend her Saturday pocket-money joy-riding on
the Metropolitan Line. She trained as a teacher and was then
called to work in South America.

Her first impression of the Indians at Mision Chaqueña
was not too good:

> They seemed scruffy and dirty and I wasn't sure if I could
> love them! The heat was awful and I had a cold . . . there
> were masses of insects. One of the first things I remember
> was a Sunday-school outing to the river – I couldn't think
> of anything worse in the middle of a tropical summer's
> day. There were lovely things, though, to cheer me up:
> the cactus flowers, the woodland by the rivers. Francis
> Tompkins [son of Alfred Tompkins] was at Mision
> Chaqueña with his wife, Jean, and Mr Everitt was there as
> well.

Francis Tompkins, who was mission superintendent for
some years, had grown up with the Indians and so was
completely in tune with them. He listened to them and
understood them. He had to leave because of overwork and
ill health.

Barbara Kitchen continues:

> I remember Mr Everitt in his peaked cap meeting me at
> Embarcacion when I arrived, and driving the car through
> the mud like Jehu! Henry and Olive Grubb were still there,
> too. Henry was very much the older-style missionary –

very correct, very silent, addressing everyone as Mr and Miss. There was little discussion – he decided what must be done and we did it. When the 'old guard' left, things became more democratic. I am so glad though that I overlapped with them. They set standards of dedication, hard work and thorough understanding of the Indians which I was able to pass on.

I had spells of work at Mison El Toba with Mr Leake, and also at San Patricio and Pozo Yacaré. Then in 1959 I joined two other new missionaries, John and Esther Bradberry, on a tour of the whole area in their jeep. This trip made me aware of the many little villages needing help, but I wasn't able to give it, as I was stationed at one place. I felt that perhaps the time had come to try to be available to more people – to be an enabler and to help the Indians who were trying to lead their own people in the schools and so on.

They needed supplies – chalk, exercise-books, pencils, paper, reading-books. Mule-cart travel wasn't satisfactory for covering the large distances involved. My home church in Watford wonderfully provided me with a vehicle and in 1962 I began a travelling ministry, assessing the needs wherever I went and trying to meet them where possible. I was based first at Mision Chaqueña and then at Juarez. Lois Cumming, a nurse, came with me and gave injections and other medical help. She also trained the Indians in dispensing simple medicines themselves. I prepared reading books in Mataco for use in the schools, and ran courses for the teachers to help them in their work.

Most villages would only have a very simple school-room – possibly only the rear-end of the church. Equipment would be not much more than a blackboard, some chalk, and a few pictures pinned to the mud walls with cactus thorns. The teacher would be a Christian, chosen by the church, and as well as Scripture, reading and writing, he would teach a little arithmetic and Argentine history and geography, and perhaps some general knowledge, depending on what he knew himself. Barbara saw her role as helping these Indian teachers by providing both equipment and training for them. In areas where there was a national school nearby she began, too, to encourage the parents to send their children there, and tried to act where possible as an intermediary between Indian families and the national schools, as integration was not always problem-free.

It was at about this time that various things happened which gave the work of God in the Argentine Chaco just the 'second wind' that it was needing. The expression is apt, as clearly the Breath of God, the Holy Spirit, was blowing where it would. For one thing, in 1958 the Lambeth Conference of bishops from the worldwide Anglican Communion declared in its report that in Latin America

> vast masses of people owe no allegiance to the Catholic Church and are a prey to materialism, secularism and to distorted forms of the Christian faith . . . so far as the Anglican Communion is concerned, South America is the neglected continent . . . South America offers a challenge and opportunity to the Anglican Communion as a great field for evangelistic work. There is every reason why it should assume larger responsibilities there.

This was quite different from the conclusion of the Edinburgh Conference of 1910, which had stated that apart from work among the indigenous Indians, the evangelism of South America must be left to the Roman Catholic Church; and as Bishop Cyril Tucker has pointed out, this difference reflects great change within the Catholic Church itself. It was now prepared to admit that there were masses of people to all intents and purposes outside the Church; it was prepared to admit that other Churches – and notably the Anglican – had a duty, if not a right, to proclaim the Gospel; and it was prepared to admit that something could be done on a united front to attempt to bring the Gospel with its healing power for the whole man to the millions with 'no hope, and without God in the world'.

And Cyril Tucker quotes the Bishop of Avellaneda, at that time head of the Episcopal Conference of all the Catholic bishops in Latin America for relations between the Churches, as saying to him one day at lunch: 'The task in South America today is more than my Church can do, it is more than your Church can do, it is more than all the Churches can do . . . and we must do it together!'

Also in 1960 a lively new general secretary was appointed to SAMS – Canon Harry Sutton, who determined to make the most of this new attitude to South America. In 1961 he visited the Argentine Chaco, and commented:

Entering the Chaco was a strange experience. I felt the utmost respect for those pioneer missionaries who had travelled this way alone on horseback. One moment we were in dense forest and the next in monotonous open scrubland; an incredible bounty of exotic birds added colour and variety. Travelling through the Argentine Chaco made such a deep impression on me that I could never be quite the same again. If I needed any extra incentive to further the work of SAMS in Latin America, I received it then. Both the poverty of the people and the courage of the Christian community had to be seen to be believed.

I was acutely conscious, too, of the sacrifices made by the missionaries and their children. I almost felt afraid for them. Apart from the emotional stress of living amid such squalor, the stifling heat, the flies, the bugs, the lack of adequate diet meant that so much of their time was taken up with the basic art of survival.

A clear pattern for the future emerged as my time in Northern Argentina drew to a close. The programme of direct evangelism and church building must continue. But it was clear that a new and enlarged medical work, together with intensive agricultural projects, was urgently required. I was appalled to see at first hand the effects of widespread malnutrition. Never shall I forget the experience of attending the funeral of the baby of a Christian

Indian family who had died as a result of malnutrition. If ever I needed encouragement to go back to Britain and continue my work for SAMS, my visit to Northern Argentina provided it. I knew that Christian mission was going to consume my life from now on.[19]

The result of this trip was a bold forward move for SAMS, with the hope of recruiting forty-five new missionaries for South America over the next three years. The forward move caught on – the Church in England was just ready for it – and in fact the Argentine Chaco alone received about forty new workers during the 1960s. This influx of new workers, and their new way of looking at things, provided the spur which the Church in the Chaco needed at that time.

Instead of sending the missionaries in ones and twos to work in comparative isolation in the various villages, the work was now based at three main centres: Algarrobal (Mision Chaqueña), La Paz and Juarez, and there the missionaries organised training courses for the Indians as well as setting out from these bases for supportive visits to the Christian settlements. New work was started in Embarcacion as well, among the Chaco Indians, who were drifting more and more into the towns and living rootlessly as the flotsam and jetsam of society there.

With so many new missionaries all coming at once, the work of God could have suffered a damaging break in continuity in the 1960s which would not have helped the Indian community, were it not for the remarkable fact that the Leake family – Alfred who had retired from the mission in 1957 and was now vicar of Guist in Norfolk, Dorothy who had returned to England in 1954 to give the children the chance of college education, and their younger daughter Dorothy – all felt called by God to go back to the Chaco.

Alfred recalls that

I was sitting in my study one day, reading the SAMS magazine which had come in the post. I read how with the Grubbs and the Dicksons both having left Argentina

(Henry Grubb after 37 years of faithful work as teacher, preacher, administrator, first rate though unqualified doctor, engineer, musician and much else), there were no senior missionaries left. Dorothy called me out to the kitchen for coffee, and I said something about the problems I had been reading about in the Chaco. 'Why don't we go back?' she said. Dorothy junior was there – she was working in a home for the mentally handicapped in Norwich. She said, 'I'll come, too!' And so in 1962 we went back.

Dorothy worked on various projects, and married Philip Miller, whom she had met at theological college, at Algarrobal.

The Leakes were to form an invaluable bridge from the small pioneering beginnings of missionary work in the Argentine Chaco which, laid on a firm foundation, had grown and prospered to the much larger and expanding structure now to be laid on those foundations. They did work on Scripture translation, based at Mision El Toba for a while, and then took charge of the new mission centre at Juarez, a centre from which Barbara Kitchen, Lois Cumming and new missionaries Walter and Sally Robbins organised educational, medical and spiritual support for the Indian villages.

In October 1963 to their great joy they welcomed their son David, now ordained, and his wife Rachel and baby son Andrew, who joined them in the work. As David and Rachel wrote in their first prayer-letter home,

The intention is that this centre should serve as a place from which we can visit the Indians along both rivers and also those who come to the railway villages seeking employment. Although the Indians on many of the mission stations have assumed a large amount of responsibility for their own churches, they still look to the missionaries for help, guidance and encouragement. A priority matter for prayer is that we may be guided very carefully in this stage of the development of the indigenous Church, that we may know what to prepare the Indians for.

The questions one has to try to answer are: Will the Indians be finally absorbed into the Argentine community or will they for ever remain a small underprivileged community who will resist absorption and remain in their huts by the rivers fishing and hunting and doing an occasional odd job for the Argentinian settlers? Whatever the answer is, and for one tribe it will be one thing and for others another, the Christian Church is committed to stand by them to help and support them, and above all whatever circumstance they may be in to relate it to the life and teaching of Jesus Christ.

Colin, studying at the Algarrobal Bible Institute.

19
A Weaning Process

Maurice Jones was nervous. The tall young Welshman was due to meet his girlfriend, Anna, that evening. He had begun to think seriously of engagement, but he would probably blow his chances when he told her what had happened to him the night before.

South America had first been brought to his attention in his theological college days, when two of his friends, Tom Curtis and Michael Vernon, were always talking about it. What is more, they not only talked and prayed, they had gone – Tom to Chile, Michael to found a Bible Institute for Indians far away in the north of Argentina. Now, in 1960, Harry Sutton, full of enthusiasm, had come to show slides of Argentina at the church in North London where Maurice was curate, and at once he had realised that God was calling him to go. In a daze, 'stingy Welshman' though he was he had shovelled every penny he had on him into the offering plate – something must have hit him pretty hard.

Although it was wonderful to know God's plan so clearly, he wondered how Anna would take it. Small, dark, tough, intelligent and gifted, she had fought against this 'Jesus person' for years, while desperately seeking the truth to live by, when suddenly at 17 God spoke and Jesus revealed to her, 'I am the truth'. Soon he had begun to show her that he might be calling her to work for him abroad; he had even given her a passionate interest in South America from childhood, but she had never linked the two in her mind. Now, when Maurice told her of his call, everything came together and she rejoiced again in the kindness of God in making her to want his will from the age of 11.

But where exactly were they to go? Maurice was convinced it was to the Algarrobal Bible Institute, but Michael Vernon had forestalled him there. Soon a letter came from SAMS saying that he was to join Alfred Leake in work among the Tobas. His heart sank. This wasn't what God had called him to at all, but in 1963 he and Anna, now married and with Rebecca their first child, prepared to go. Six weeks before they were due to sail they heard that Judy Vernon's health had broken down and she and Michael were leaving Algarrobal for Buenos Aires at once. Maurice and Anna went to Algarrobal, moved straight into the Vernons' house and started work.

After a slow start, the school began to fill up with students from the banks of the Pilcomayo and Bermejo Rivers: 'By train, bicycle and on foot they came. One group walked for five days to reach the railway line and then, unable to afford the train fare, begged a lift in the truck of a cargo train. Shabbily and raggedly dressed, barefooted or with toes poking out of rope-soled shoes, they looked unlikely candidates, but of their enthusiasm there was never any doubt.'

Lois Cumming, who wrote this account, also observed the spiritual calibre of the students:

After preaching at a nearby service, a visit was made to a sick lad of about 14 by three of the students. What struck me most was their love and concern for the boy's spiritual welfare: 'Have you prayed to God to make you better?' asked Mario, their leader, as they stood round the rough bed. Then shaking his head rather sadly he added, 'I don't think he knows how to pray,' and followed this with a simple explanation of how to turn to Christ with our physical and spiritual needs. Then after prayer and a word to the parents on their duty to teach their son the elements of the Christian faith, they left.

Soon people trained at the Institute began to make a considerable contribution to the life of the church in the Chaco, as when an Australian missionary, Kevin Bewley, had at the last moment to withdraw from giving a series of lectures at a proposed Bible School course at La Paz, and Alberto from San Andres cycled sixty miles to give in his place excellent lectures on the Ten Commandments and the history of Israel. The students at the Algarrobal Bible Institute were those Indians who had already emerged as leaders in their villages, and in order to be accepted in the Institute they had to have the backing of their own church.

They did manual work on the upkeep of the property and in the agricultural schemes to pay for their keep. Once their studies were finished, they had to continue to show their commitment and leadership ability in their home churches before they could be ordained. The older men were mostly ordained on merit, without studying at the school – they would not have coped with pens and paper very well. Alfred Leake helped with the Bible Institute for some time, concentrating on teaching the Toba men.

Maurice Jones has some splendid stories about those years. One was a mystery. One of the students, a man called Mariano Centeno, was unwell. Gradually over a period of eighteen months he became thin, depressed and lifeless and no one could find out what was wrong. Heart trouble? Stomach? The doctors could diagnose nothing, but the man just was not ticking over at all. Maurice began to fear he would give up the course, when suddenly he became himself again – his confidence returned, he began eating and putting on weight.

One day he told Maurice what had happened. A local witch-doctor had a wife who was a Christian. Despite her Christian faith, this woman was encouraging people to go to her husband for witch-doctoring for financial gain. Mariano, as a member of the church council, had to rebuke the woman and tell her she could not come to the Lord's Table while this was going on. As a result, the witch-doctor put a curse on Mariano's family and worry had caused his illness. Knowing nothing of this, Maurice, in the course of the Old Testament studies at the college, had been expounding the story of Gideon in Judges chapter 6 – how *although he was afraid, Gideon obeyed*. It was this truth which had freed Mariano from the fear and power of the witch-doctor which had been crippling him for eighteen months.

Another story Maurice tells is of a pastoral trip he undertook early in 1964 when he was still fairly new to the Chaco, together with Kevin Bewley and an Indian lay preacher called Urbano:

We were visiting a small railway village called Basan and on our first night, after chatting with the small number of faithful Christians, we had retired to our sleeping-bags under the cold, clear, starlit winter sky. Soon we heard the weird and frightening sound of the witch-doctors' rattles and bells and chanting, apparently very close. We got up and dressed, and after Kevin had encouraged us by reading from Ephesians about 'the whole armour of God', we walked in the direction of the sound. Not far away we found a circle of 50–60 people with a log fire in the middle and a sick woman lying on the ground near the fire. Two witch-doctors, naked except for loin-cloths, bells on chest and back, feathers on knees, wrists and ankles and a gourd rattle in each hand were dancing frenziedly round the woman, chanting and hissing breath out of their lungs in an effort to drive the evil spirits away. They were brothers – two tractor-drivers who worked on the white men's tomato plantations.

A way was made for our missionary party to come to the centre of the ring and some, who were supposedly Christians, slipped hastily away – the really faithful ones were not there anyway.

'Stop!' shouted Kevin in Mataco, and they did.

'Who are you, and what are you doing?'

'We are sons of the devil, and we are driving away the evil spirits that are causing this sickness.'

'Listen to the word of the Lord,' Kevin replied, and he began reading Acts chapter 13 about Paul defying Elymas the magician. He had only read a few verses when the witch-doctors started up again, drowning Kevin's reading with their noise. Undeterred, Kevin turned to Urbano and me and told us to get down on our knees. The people looked from the witch-doctors to us and back again, wondering what would happen, and Kevin prayed quietly but earnestly for the Lord to show his love and mercy to these people, to stop them and to show them their need of Christ. As he prayed, it was as though the strength drained away from the two witch-doctors before us.

Kevin finished his prayer amid silence, the only other sound that of the two witch-doctors panting as though they had run a marathon – shoulders slumped, arms loose by their sides. We got up and Kevin read from Acts 13 again. This time it was listened to in silence and then Kevin preached on the rest of the chapter – the love of Christ shown on the Cross, and the need to repent and turn to him. When he had finished preaching, he turned to us and said simply, 'Let's go', and the three of us turned and walked away. The noise started up again, but soon petered out. This happened several times – they couldn't get going, somehow, and eventually at dawn we heard them drive away by tractor.

In the morning we went to the sick woman's house. She was very nice – an older Christian, as was her husband. The witch-doctors were their unbelieving sons who had forced the 'treatment' on her. She told us that as she lay helplessly on the ground she had been praying for the Lord to intervene. We had no idea during the dramatic events of that evening that we were the answer to her prayer. Later, with Lois's help, we were able to give her medical aid. One faithful Christian at Basan who was greatly encouraged by the power of God shown that evening was Francisco Lopez who became an outstanding student at the Institute.

One other story of Maurice Jones concerns a pastoral trip which he made later with Mario Mariño to the churches south of the Bermejo. These churches had been formed without any missionary evangelism or oversight as a result of visits to Pozo Yacaré by Christians in the 1940s and '50s. The only missionary who had visited these places – Sauzal,

Saucelito, Nuevo Pompeya, so far was Lois Cumming, and now Maurice and Mario were going – Maurice the first ordained person to visit them – for a pastoral, teaching and baptising ministry.

David Leake took us from Juarez to the north bank of the Bermejo and then we were taken across the river in a canoe made from the hollowed-out trunk of a bottle tree. As we set off, the boatman announced, 'The boat tipped over yesterday' (not surprisingly – it had no keel); 'We're still looking for the body.' The passengers prayed earnestly for safety – especially as Maurice had never learnt to swim. (He recalls, too, a more recent crossing in 1986, when on a pitch-dark night they crossed by the light of Halley's comet shining reddish-gold on the black water of the Bermejo.)

Once across we proceeded by donkey. The animals were stubborn and we threatened to turn them into corned beef if they didn't get moving. We travelled three or four days with our feet either almost touching the ground or if in the stirrups with our knees touching our chins. At Sauzal we conducted services and baptisms and borrowed bicycles for the final stretch to Nueva Pompeya. There were soft sandy areas where we had to carry the bikes, and dry bits where the bumpy imprints of the cattle's hooves set our teeth chattering. It was November and the temperature was 105 or 106°F in the shade. Exhausted, we stopped and slumped over the handlebars of our bikes. There was blood on the road where a puma had dragged a deer along. Vultures hovered above us waiting for the remains of the deer. On our left was a little wayside cemetery. Looking at all these ominous signs, Mario joked, 'The vultures are ready for us!'

At Nueva Pompeya we found a church which had been in existence for over twenty years and had never been visited by an ordained man. On our first night there – a Saturday – we were teaching and singing hymns with them until very late – they just wanted more and more. That day, too, Mario and I interviewed forty-six candidates for baptism – they were baptised the next day.

We were thrilled with the spiritual depth of these people. We held a communion service, too, the newly baptised joining in, together with some of the church leaders who had already been confirmed at Pozo Yacaré. There being little likelihood of an early visit by a bishop, I made use of the clause in the 1662 Prayer Book allowing communion to those who are 'ready and desirous of confirmation'.

So, for nine years, in the course of which Maurice made a first-ever translation of selections of the Old Testament from Genesis to Malachi, but arranged in historical order of events, Maurice and Anna worked on at Algarrobal. Maurice also, together with Pat Harris, worked on Mataco liturgies and on a book of pastoral guidelines for the newly ordained Indian leaders. While there, Anna made the drawings which illustrate this book.

A new medical centre was also developing at La Paz under the leadership of Dr Michael Patterson and Nurse Helen Sohns. Michael and Virginia Patterson had come to Argentina, newly married, in 1963, and found the mission 'very small, very insular, very isolated', with Francis Tompkins in charge, overworked and far from well. Soon they were sent to La Paz, their task being to set up the third of the new main centres of the mission.

Over the previous few years missionaries had had to withdraw from La Paz because of the shortage of workers, and a Choroti Indian called David Gonzalez had been shepherding the church, with a helper called Lorenzo who ran the school. Both had been well trained by Harry Dickson, writing, for example, in a beautiful copper-plate hand which they had learnt from him. There was little medical work, although Helen Sohns, a calm and competent nurse, was already working in the area when the Pattersons arrived.

Michael soon realised that the time for a purely expatriate set-up was past. He went to the local provincial ministry of

health and put it to them like this: 'Here we are, willing to
help, but we want to work in your way and with your
support. Can you supply us with drugs and give us a salary?'

They liaised, too, with the Flying Doctor, who had already
been paying monthly visits to La Paz but concentrating
largely on the settler population, and on these visits they
arranged for the delivery of the drugs they needed as well as
for transport of patients where necessary. Helen Sohns soon
started nursing courses, to train the Indians to deal with
simple cases themselves, and eventually these, too, came
under the auspices of the government, with a course run in
Tartagal entirely for Indian students.

Once trained, these Indian nurses went back to their
villages and worked for the government there, and Michael
and Helen's role became primarily that of supervision and
support. From their base at La Paz they would go off on
ten-day safaris, advising the village nurses, particularly on
difficult cases, taking supplies, and concentrating on pre-
ventative medicine. Immunisations were introduced against
measles and whooping cough, and as Michael remembers,
'even the witch-doctor would send his children for those!'

Malaria had been largely eradicated by government-
sponsored DDT-spraying since the 1950s, but as well as
syphilis, brucellosis, chagas disease and internal parasites,
TB was still a serious problem and a 'hospital village' was
built at La Paz where long-term TB patients and their
families could stay. Serious cases encountered on the supportive safaris would be brought back to La Paz and flown to
the hospital at Tartagal. It is interesting to note, too, that the
medical work was greatly helped at this time by the provision
of a new pick-up vehicle bought with money raised at a
'Tear Fund' concert in England at which Cliff Richard
sang.

Eventually the Pattersons moved to Embarcacion and
later to Salta, as Michael was made head of the mission's
whole medical team of trained nurses, doctors and (later)
dentists who worked among the Indians in the Argentine
Chaco. Another role which the missionaries developed in the

towns was that of intermediary between sick Indians in hospital and the Spanish-speaking medical staff.

As Doreen Maxwell-Jones remembers, 'Some of the Indians were terrified of the hospital, and convinced that the doctors wanted to kill them. Speaking their language, we would seek to reassure them and to help them to explain to the nurses what they wanted. Once when we were told that "there was no spare bed" for a needy Indian patient, we simply marched in with a bed to the hospital!'

Also based at La Paz while the Pattersons were there was the Rev. Pat Harris, a new recruit from Oxford, who paid pastoral visits to the Indian settlements on horseback. Converted at a Crusader Camp at the age of 15, he had read law at Oxford and then studied for the ministry, being ordained in 1960. At the start of his three-year curacy at St Ebbe's Church, Oxford, he prayed, 'Lord, at the end of these three years I'm willing to go anywhere and do anything for you. Please make your will plain during this time.'

In December, 1960, an old friend wrote to say that SAMS were holding a conference in Oxford which he wanted to go to, and could Pat put him up? Pat decided to go with his friend to the conference, and so God began to answer his prayer and to call him to South America, a call that was confirmed in various ways. Even a map, left in a drawer of an old desk he had been given, turned out to be of South America!

After three months' studying of Mataco at Mision Chaqueña, Pat arrived at La Paz in 1963, the first ordained man to live and work among the Indians on the northern reaches of the Pilcomayo. With many senior missionaries having left, it was clear to the young missionaries who were now coming out – too new to the language and the ways of the people to be able to take much leadership themselves – that responsibility for the churches should now be in the hands of the Indians; the missionaries' role from now on must be primarily a 'weaning process' – that of teaching and equipping the Indian lay evangelists to take full leadership themselves. At first Pat, as the only ordained man in the area, travelled a great deal, visiting the churches and administering the sacraments, but he felt more and more strongly that it was wrong to appear in the role of a sort of 'mass priest' with special powers, when the Indians should be seeking ordination so that they could administer the sacraments themselves.

At any rate, he set himself with a will to getting to know the Indians as he travelled among them, taking no special supplies with him on his travels, living as they lived, eating what they ate and sharing their maté as they drank round the fire together. Soon he came to love them very much: Mariano at Santa Teresa who would welcome him with such a warm embrace as he rode into the village that he felt as if he were coming home; Carlos, the converted witch-doctor from Santa Maria who was now the pastor at Poso Tigre – a gracious, godly, simple man; David Gonzalez and his son, Felipe, at La Paz; Lorenzo also at La Paz and many others.

With David Gonzalez and his brother Anselmo, Pat also paid a five-day visit to Santa Maria where they were welcomed, as Pat put it, 'with open arms and plenty of fish'. They found the village much in need of advice and help and strong Christian leadership, with things made harder for the Christians by the presence not only of many Spanish-speaking Argentines in the area, but also of a government nurse who was a strong Roman Catholic and unfortunately unsympathetic and indeed opposed to the Anglican work. While there, Pat called on Pablo and had talks with him, finding him fearful of the pain and difficulty which it would cost to come back to the Lord.

Until now hymns for the village services had mostly been set to English tunes, Indian music being rhythmical rather than tuneful, but on a trip to Buenos Aires Pat first heard hymns being sung to lively Latin-American tunes. He introduced this new music to the Indians back in the Chaco, teaching Felipe Gonzalez to play the guitar and playing a piano-accordion of Barbara Kitchen's himself. It caught on at once, and now groups play this music all over the Chaco, a great asset to the worship everywhere.

Carlos left Pozo Tigré, where he had been evangelist and teacher for fourteen years, at about this time and moved back to his original home of San Luis, and Pat explained the sad reason for this in one of his prayer-letters home:

Carlos has endured a great deal patiently, and his decision to leave was no hurried one, but was made under the guidance of the Holy Spirit. In recent months opposition has increased; two gardens he had made were spoiled and the fences removed; twice he was threatened with a knife; his TB pills were stolen from his home. But the two hardest things to bear were first to see his youngest son, a lad of about 15, gradually influenced by his companions, and to see him drunk and addicted to coca; and second the agony of living in such surroundings where many have heard and rejected the Gospel, and no longer have any shame at committing the lewdest sins openly. Pat described vividly how after prayer, Carlos left for San Luis, taking with him the church bell (a piece of railway line), and the black-board. As Pat commented, 'They won't be needed now that Carlos, the evangelist and school-teacher, has gone away; but the people still need a Saviour.'

The Christians at La Paz became very aware at this time of the need to reach out to their *Criollo* neighbours, of whom there were many around Santa Maria and La Paz, and they began holding services in Spanish for them. Indeed during the 1960s the outreach of the Anglican Church in the whole area of Northern Argentina took on a new dimension, as instead of working only among the Indians, its members, both missionary and Indian, gained confidence in sharing the Gospel with their Spanish-speaking 'white' neighbours as well.

This development was mirrored in the towns, so that in 1969 Pat Harris and his wife Valerie were able to write home,

The work among the Spanish-speaking people here in the north is most encouraging, especially in Embarcacion under Walter and Sally Robbins. During the eighteen months of its existence, the church has grown and flourished. Just last week the whole church moved en bloc to Juarez (34 of them) to lead a weekend campaign. Two folk who happened to drop in to the counselling classes in Embarcacion were converted.

In May, we held a service for the Spanish-speaking people in La Paz, and eight said they wished to commit their lives to Christ. Also Pat has recently twice visited the village of Hickman where a local railwayman has been converted through the witness of the local Indian pastor.

The small town of Hickman lies on the railway line between Embarcacion and Formosa, the *Criollo* community living on the main street with its stores, first-aid post and school, and the houses of the Indians standing a little apart, clustered round the church and evangelist's house on the other side of the railway line.

In the 1960s a small group of *Criollo* cowboys and their wives from the nearby village of San Martin were converted through the witness of a Christian Indian who gave one of them a Spanish Bible. As a result, they and the Indians became good friends, having first become brothers in Christ. As Lois Cumming commented at the time, 'Look at Don Nicolas, for example, who will even bring a sick Indian the nine and a half miles to Mision Chaqueña for treatment and then offer to pay for it! Such a thing is unheard of, but typical of the change that conversion has made in these men.'

So the 'wind of change' which had been given formal expression at the Lambeth Conference in 1958, was becoming a living reality in the towns and villages of the Argentine Chaco.

20

The First Ordinations

Other important developments for the Church took place during the 1960s. In 1963 a consultation on 'The Anglican Communion and South America' was convened at Cuerna-vaca, Mexico, one result of which was the dividing of the southern part of South America, apart from Brazil, into two new dioceses and the appointment of the Rev. Cyril Tucker as Bishop of the diocese of Argentina and Eastern South America with the Falkland Islands. He writes of that time:

One of the 'raw' – if not young – recruits arriving for the Chaco work was myself as Bishop! True, I had taken an honours degree in Anthropology at Cambridge which meant learning a great deal about primitive peoples and their religion; and I had been through all my ministry greatly committed to the mission of the Church, with close links with the Church Missionary Society and its work in Africa and the East. I was well aware of modern mission-ary thinking and the principles of church growth and the establishment of indigenous churches. But I had every-thing to learn about the Chaco and its Indians, and it was mostly from Alfred Leake that I learnt it. Protracted tours round the Chaco with Alfred (and also with his son, David, born among the Indians) taught me not only so much about the Indians, but also a great deal about the whole history and life of the mission in the Chaco and the sterling character and worth of the pioneer missionaries. This is not to detract from the help, care and wonderful welcome I received from all the other missionaries, most of whom, one must say, had learnt a great deal about the Chaco in a remarkably short time. I have very many happy and hallowed memories of our fellowship together in Christ in the proclamation of the Gospel, and in the adventurous journeys I made together with them.

As he travelled round the Chaco with Alfred, Cyril Tucker thought deeply about the possibility of the ordination of Indians to the ministry of the Anglican Church. It was a need of which the missionaries had been aware for many years, aware though they were, too, of the risks. Cyril Tucker looks back to that time, and to how their thinking went, as they pondered the question together.

The work of God's Spirit through the work of the missionaries over the years had resulted in many transformed and radiant Christian lives. Moreover, there were scattered throughout the Indian villages fine men of God who were showing great Christian leadership and exhibiting real pastoral gifts. They were taking services, preaching and praying with Spirit-given power, all based on a sound knowledge of such parts of the Bible as were available to them. The guidance was clear: although these men had no formal education or special training, their full commitment to Christ and the witness they were making gave them, in my opinion, all the qualifications needed for ordination in the Anglican Church. The passage of Scripture most in my mind at this time was Acts, Chapter 10, verses 47 and 48 where Peter asks – when there is evident working of the Holy Spirit – why should not these be baptised? *Mutatis mutandis*, one asked, 'Why should these men not be ordained?' I could find answers to that question, but none seemed valid!

Alfred, from his long experience, was careful to put the other side: He could look back over the years and recall how seemingly strong Indian Christians had fallen away; but is not this a sad fact in every part of the Christian Church . . . and among clergy, too! How right it was for Alfred to raise such questions, and because of his long experience he was able – and characteristically good and great enough – to give invaluable help in framing measures designed, under God, to fend off failure. For I had every intention of following St Paul's instruction to Timothy, 'Lay hands suddenly on no man.' Much preparation, as well as prayer, was necessary.

First, it was not just the Bishop or the missionaries who decided whom to ordain; nor was it just the men themselves believing that they had been called to this ministry. They were being ordained to continue in a new and enhanced way their local ministry in their village, and the local church needed to be involved in their selection. Alfred had made it clear to me that unless the ordinand was chosen and fully accepted by those among whom he lived, his ministry could not be fully effective. Of course this was not just a question of 'efficient' ministry. To my mind it corresponded to the practice of the primitive Church and also tested the life and character of the men in a way that no 'outside' testing or questioning could. Alfred, who had known these men and the village congregations over many years, in a way that newer missionaries could not, was therefore a fundamental help in this matter.

Many other important matters had to be discussed, such as the form of Prayer Book to be used. Cyril Tucker was well aware of the temptation 'in the name of indigenisation' to introduce or leave things out, things which suited particular people or situations rather than reflecting the doctrine and beliefs of the Anglican Church. It seemed to him that

We must not let 'indigenisation' mean our behaving like Baptists or Brethren or Presbyterians. This is not to say that we do not learn from them, or that we are right and others wrong. It is saying that almost the only justification for us to be in South America at all is that we believe the Anglican way is not only different from other ways, but has a specific contribution to make within the variety of other expressions in the continent. If we simply adopt, or adapt to, these other ways, we fail to make our specific contribution. This is a question still being faced by the growing Anglican churches in South America.

At any rate the good hand of our God was upon us, and all was happily agreed and arranged. At the Ordination Retreats I was able to speak personally (by interpretation) to each candidate and to pray with him. This brought a real assurance that all (except one, I think) were truly 'called', so that the Ordination Services were a most tremendous time for praise and dedication for the whole Church in the Chaco, and we are still thanking God for all that this has meant for the blessing of the Church through its growth and extension.

In fact the first ordination of Indians took place in April 1966, those ordained by Bishop Tucker being Carlos of San Luis, David of La Paz, and Samuel, Ernesto, Marciano, Colin and Mariano of Desmontes. They wore their best clothes, but even so were a motley crowd, with Carlos for instance resplendent in a white skirt made out of an old table-cloth (Carlos always wore the old traditional men's skirt) and a Marks and Spencer pyjama jacket by way of a shirt. To Alfred Leake,

> the service (conducted for the very first time in Mataco) in the rustic church of La Paz was very impressive. Dorothy and I were so very glad that the way opened up for us to be present, and that I was able to take part in the service. Having come to the Chaco when only one mission existed, it was a great thrill to represent, as it were, our older colleagues who did so much in the founding of the missions and the building up of the work in the Argentine Chaco. What a joy it was also to see men, most of whom I had known for many years, ordained to a fuller ministry among their own people.

Indeed, Alfred's presence and his preparation of the candidates expressed vividly to the Indians that the ordinations were a natural development of the growth of their Church, and were not just an idea of the newer missionaries.

21
Material Needs – a Ten Year Plan

As well as his glad recognition of the spiritual growth of the Church in the Chaco, the other thing left with Cyril Tucker on his travels, less happily, was a sense of shock at the dismayingly low physical and material state of the Indians:

> little food, much illness, high incidence of infant mortality, still very primitive shelters to live in. It is not too much to say that many of the conditions I had experienced while spending three and a half years as a prisoner of war of the Japanese were recalled to my mind! I remember a missionary who confided to me that he thought conditions had indeed grown worse in the three years he spent there around 1960. Conditions were, I would judge, better in the earlier days of missionary work in the Chaco, as the Indians were still able to exist off the land and goats had not yet produced barrenness nor had various exploitations begun.

It is hard to pinpoint the cause of the worsening of the material condition of the Indians: uncertainties in the sugar industry which meant that they might suddenly find that they were not needed one season, the ruination of the grass-land caused by goats of both squatters and Indians, the cutting down of forest-land (thousands of quebracho trees being felled for railway-sleepers and the tannin they contained) and many other factors all contributed. As Alfred Leake commented,

> This is far too great a problem for the mission to tackle as a whole, although the rustic chair industry, commenced many years ago by Mr Everitt, was still going strong, and

the buying and selling of weaving, string work, Indian weapons and so on is a great help. But the basic problem remains and has been accentuated in recent years by lack of rain, apparent falling off of fish supplies, and wider tastes both in matters of food and clothing since the Indians have come more into contact with civilisation.

In 1967 Alfred expressed the problem even more forcibly:

We feel that a critical stage has been reached in the long period of transition for the Chaco Indians. Much as many of them, and especially the older generation, would prefer to stay permanently and undisturbed in their old haunts, pursuing their old way of life as a 'hunting and gathering' people, this is yearly becoming more difficult. A dwindling rainfall and unrestrained cattle which break into gardens are causing would-be gardeners to lose heart. The river seems to be in a state of being gradually 'fished out'. Game is getting more scarce and some animals and reptiles which Indians have always killed with impunity are now protected game. Marauding cattle spoil much of the forest fruit as soon as it falls to the ground and before the women have a chance to gather it up.

The tendency is to come to town when hunger and the need for clothes become too pressing. But this is not the answer, as anyone who has passed the last two or three months in a place like Juarez readily sees. The whole question needs a great deal of wisdom and careful handling. Many Indians are becoming bewildered and inclined to turn anywhere where help may be forthcoming. We can only thank God that there are so many Christians among them and that many of them are men of sound common sense. How we thank God for them all and praise Him that the Gospel reached so many thousands of these Indian peoples before these critical days which we now see.

It was at about this time that the material problems of the Indians first attracted widespread attention in Argentina, being featured in the national newspapers and on television. For example, an article by Michael Mainwaring in the *Buenos Aires Herald* of 1969, entitled 'The Forgotten Argentines', began as follows:

> The man in the street – and even the man in authority – doesn't know, possibly doesn't want to know, much about the 10,000 Indians living in the Argentine Chaco. From the comfort and distance of Buenos Aires it is easy for government and people alike to ignore death and misery on the Pilcomayo. When it is learnt that Englishmen have been working with them since 1914 it is easy to spread rumours: 'The imperialistic English are pressing in upon Argentina from two sides: from the Malvinas in the South and the Chaco in the North.' It is easy to criticise someone who is doing a job that you know you should be doing yourself.

After describing the missionaries' work and some of the difficulties, the article ends with this challenge: 'And worst of all, the missionaries realise that the biggest battle is fast becoming a losing one – to persuade the Argentine people to accept these Indians as human beings, and the Argentine government to accept some sort of responsibility for looking after them.'

As a result of this publicity a census was taken, the Indians began to be more widely registered and given full rights of Argentine citizenship, and various plans were afoot regarding their welfare. Tons of food were distributed by the government, and even wire-netting to enable them to fence in the land on which they lived. In fact much more food *wasn't* properly distributed; some was left lying around to rot, and one policeman left the police force and started up a store with all the food he was supposed to distribute.

A new problem now arose for the missionaries in that, as the only people who spoke the Indian languages and enjoyed their confidence, they were called upon to help with these projects for social aid – something they were more than

happy to do as long as their involvement did not deflect them
from their primary call to minister the Gospel. One example
of this was David Leake's setting up (at the provincial
government's request) of the Juarez Social Project in 1965 –
soon after he and Rachel came to work with the mission.

In many ways it was a headache: trying to reconcile the
ideas of the government department of social welfare with
what he knew of the culture of the people themselves; trying
to organise and restrain the radical young men who had been
sent to help; rendering accounts which were not only correct
but also tallied with the government's original proposals. It
was this, Rachel reckons, that turned David's hair prema-
turely grey – so difficult was it to run this social project as well
as pastoring the people.

Cyril Tucker, who himself did much to make large grants
of money from relief organisations available in the Chaco,
reflected on the double loyalty like this:

> While the newer missionaries were by and large well
> behind all the efforts to improve the material lot of the
> Indians, I believe the older generation had some hesi-
> tations that it might mean a dilution of the real work of the
> mission. I recall Alfred Leake telling me of problems when
> in the past the missionaries had started a shop to sell to the
> Indians simple necessaries at just prices: it had, he said,
> caused an awful lot of work and worry with much time
> consumed in overseeing matters.
>
> However it was not the principle – that Christ's Good
> News was for the whole man – but the practicality of it that
> he was questioning. Certainly I felt that it was neither
> an 'either/or' nor even 'both', but that there was but
> one Gospel to be proclaimed which was 'wholeness'
> (salvation) through the infinite love and grace of God in
> Christ. One proclaimed that Gospel by offering a cup of
> cold water in His name, as by quoting a verse from the
> New Testament.
>
> I have stressed this point because while my many
> friends in SAMS over the years have very kindly spoken of

my boldness in taking the memorable step of ordaining the first South American Indians, and have said that I shall inevitably be remembered for this, in my own heart – if, like St Paul, I boast as a fool – I would wish to have some credit for seeking to change the material conditions within which ministry and mission have developed.

In 1968 the Indians in the Chaco suffered from very severe flooding of the River Pilcomayo – the biggest floods within living memory. Alfred commented on an article in a leading Buenos Aires newspaper in which the writer expressed the hope that as the eyes of the nation had been turned to this poor and isolated province because of the flood, it would not be forgotten when the waters subsided and life returned to normal:

'Poor and isolated' are appropriate adjectives, and life grows ever more difficult for the Indians and poor whites here. Woodcutting has stopped completely owing to government restrictions and consequently business has slumped. The Government Petroleum Co. has pulled out after about twenty-five years of exploration. There is little or no work to be had within hundreds of miles of Juarez, and at the moment this district would appear to have no future.

In the same prayer-letter though, he rejoiced in the continuing growth of the Church, with the first two Tobas shortly to be ordained, and six more Matacos, all of whom had been through a two-year course at the Bible Institute at Algarrobal. Of the Toba ordination, he wrote,

It was fitting that David (Leake), whom they had known all their lives, should be there to preach the sermon, and that he and four Mataco pastors, not long ordained themselves, should take part in the ceremony of the laying on of hands. It was fitting also that this Toba ordination should have been taken by Bishop Tucker as almost his last act of service in the Chaco before he relinquishes oversight of this area which is soon to become part of the new diocese. He made history when he ordained the first Chaco Indians, and it is thanks to him that we now have twenty-two Indian pastors. As we look back, we bow our heads in humility and amazement, filled with awe and deep gratitude to Almighty God for all that has been accomplished since Bishop Tucker was appointed to the diocese only five years ago.

The new diocese to which Alfred here referred was to include Paraguay and five provinces of Northern Argentina. The man who was to take over as bishop was Bill Flagg, an energetic man who had managed a mission farm in Chile and had then worked with SAMS in Paraguay before coming to the Argentine Chaco in 1964. In fact he had first visited Algarrobal in 1959, when he was asked to take the Bible readings at a staff conference. When Francis Tompkins had to retire as mission superintendent, Bill Flagg took over. Later he was made archdeacon and then in 1969 bishop, with David Leake as his assistant.

Bill Flagg, David Leake and Maurice Sinclair, an agriculturalist who arrived in 1968, became much involved in a further major development in the Argentine Chaco which has already been touched on: the involvement of relief organisations in agricultural projects for the benefit of the Indians. In about 1970 three projects were launched. Two of these, financed by Christian Aid, were agricultural schemes based at La Paz and Mision Chaqueña, involving irrigation from the Pilcomayo and from a deep-bore well respectively. The hope was, by introducing irrigation techniques and increasing the scale of cultivation, to help the Indians to produce enough food to sustain them all the year round – i.e., to achieve a gradual transition from hunting and gathering to agriculture. In addition, peppers and tomatoes were grown as cash crops for sale in the cities. On the industrial side, Oxfam gave funds for a powerful diesel engine and dynamo and electrically-driven machinery to help with the carpentry work.

In 1972 a report, 'Ten Vital Years', appeared, describing plans for a coordinated programme of social outreach by the Anglican Church in the Argentine Chaco: *Iniciativa Cristiana*. This was eventually to include land purchase and settlement projects as well as the agricultural schemes, along with the original medical, educational and pastoral support for the Indians. In addition to the agencies already mentioned, considerable sums of money were given by Tear Fund, SAMS and by Argentine government departments to get these schemes started.

The stated objective was 'to identify with the Indian communities in their attempts to adapt to a situation of massive change, helping them to understand and share positively in the new culture . . . relating it to the old culture without despising that culture's traditional values.' On the one hand, the aim was to help them to continue their lives in the country areas, but with improved opportunities for agriculture and jobs; on the other hand, to help those who chose to migrate to the towns in adapting to life there.

The missionaries, working together with trained specialists, were uniquely in a position to do this. Speaking the Indian languages as they did, and identifying with them in their lives, they were able to bridge the culture gap – indeed they had been acting as intermediaries for many years – and to help the Indians and the Argentines to bridge the gap themselves.

In the realm of education, it is significant that the missionaries from the very start had taught the Indians in their own languages as well as in Spanish, whereas in the government schools only Spanish was used. A conference of anthropologists meeting in Barbados in 1971 drew attention to the danger that a powerful culture imposing itself upon a weaker one can destroy all that gives a people security and roots. They accused religious missions in Latin America of imposing alien patterns of thought upon the Indians, with the danger of their losing their own culture and the dignity that goes with it.

In fact, as Maurice Sinclair points out in his book, *Green*

Finger of God, 'the learning of a native language, its reduction into written form, and the translation of the Bible into that language is the most benign form of cultural interaction that could possibly be conceived', as education guided by Biblical insights recognises the nobility and genius in every human culture (that of those being taught as well as that of the teacher), as having been created by God.

On the economic side, the hope of the ten-year plan of the *Iniciativa Cristiana* was to make a decisive impact on the poverty in the area, and through agriculture, crafts and industry to create work opportunities in the Indians' traditional areas. The idea was to introduce agricultural cooperatives so that costly irrigation pumps and tractors could be shared beyond the extended family; but it was also recognised that plans mustn't be imposed, but must spring from the wishes of the people themselves. This was a difficult balance to maintain, but again the confidence which already existed between missionaries and local people was a great help. Farms growing both cash and subsistence crops were established at Mision La Paz and at Mision El Toba, as well as at Mision Chaqueña, but sadly the two former failed, partly because of severe flooding of the Pilcomayo, but also because these two sites were too remote from adequate roads and other amenities, so that production costs were impossibly high.

Mision Chaqueña, being nearer to civilisation, had a much better chance of success. It soon became clear that viable farms could only be established in this border zone between traditional agricultural areas and the undeveloped Chaco, and this led on to land settlement projects, where land was bought up in these border-zone areas and the Indians encouraged to move their families on to them and to work on the farms, while improved housing, schools and medical services were provided for them and for their families.

The first of these settlements was at Carboncito, a village near Mision Chaqueña. It also began to be realised, after the failure of the farm projects at La Paz and MET, that perhaps a mistake had been made in concentrating too much on cash crops and large scale machinery. Later, as a result of inflation, the Falklands War and other factors, the schemes at Algarrobal and Carboncito failed too. Prayerfully, the Christians involved had to seek God's wisdom in finding how to help the Indians best to help themselves in their changing situation, and this led them back, at least in part, to improved subsistence farming. They have always been conscious of their fallibility, and have been prepared in their ministry to the Indians to learn from and with them.

J. H. Palmer summarised the situation as he saw it in 1976 quite well: Having commented on the cultural disintegration leading to extinction which usually occurs when a group's traditional values are upset by contact with groups holding different values, he observed that

There is a paradox in the present state of development of Mataco culture. In spite of an increasing commitment to white values, the Mataco population itself is growing, thanks to the medical work of the Protestant missionaries, who have reduced the infant mortality rate and are implementing vaccination programmes against endemic tuberculosis. Much of the tribe still lives on its traditional lands in indigenous communities, and the tribe, particularly in the River Pilcomayo area, still preserves to a large extent its hunting and gathering economy, aspects of its material culture, and its language. This paradox may be partly explained by the history of relations between the Indians of the area and white society, which have undergone a process of cyclical reversion – from almost a century of labour relations based on the sugar industry, the Indians were forced to return to their traditional economy (though more limited in scope) when the sugar industry was mechanised in the early 1960s . . . The missionaries continue to support the Matacos, particularly with agricultural projects . . . That a Mataco population survives at all is due directly to missionary involvement in the area during this century.

22

Bishops' Move

The Chaco villages were changing. Even in 1971, Pat Harris going back after four years' absence to visit La Paz, where he had first worked, observed,

> Today La Paz has a large clinic with some beds for patients, a large agricultural scheme financed by Oxfam, and now this month there has been a large grant of money from the Government to provide water in the village and better housing. The change is amazing, but this has brought in its wake many problems. The big danger is that with increasing prosperity the people will lose their love for their Lord – of course this has always been a danger all the world over – from the time that the Israelites went into the Promised Land: 'Take heed lest you forget.'

In fact, any apparent increasing prosperity was very fragile, but while much effort was being put into schemes for improving the material lot of the Indians and helping them culturally to adapt to the changes which were facing them, the church in the Chaco was itself changing and soon was to be bursting with new life.

In 1973, after four immensely energetic and fruitful years as Bishop of Paraguay and Northern Argentina – years in which the Ten Year Plan had been formulated and was beginning to be put into operation – Bishop Flagg moved on to pioneer new work in Peru, and Pat Harris, who had been archdeacon since 1969 and who spoke both Mataco and Spanish, was consecrated bishop with David Leake remaining as assistant. All previous bishops had been consecrated in Buenos Aires, and none, apart of course from David Leake, had spoken an Indian language.

Pat was unhappy with the image of a bishop as someone remote and foreign, just brought in for special events, and felt strongly that he should be consecrated among the people whom he would be pastoring. He also saw clearly that sooner or later an Indian would be consecrated bishop, and he wanted his own consecration to be identical to that which such a man would have, so as to set a pattern, as well as ensuring that any subsequent consecration of an Indian would be seen by everyone to be 'the real thing'.

Pat Harris was consecrated therefore at Mision Chaqueña, wearing an open-necked shirt and a poncho. The poncho was chosen by way of a surplice as being cool, simple and serviceable, as well as being indigenous and easy to make. It was just an oblong strip of white sheeting with a hole in the middle: for clergy a black strip of ribbon is sewn down each side, and for bishops a red. The music for the service was provided by seven guitars, a Paraguayan harp, two piano-accordions and by tambourines.

Shortly after his consecration, Bishop Harris called the church leaders together for a synod meeting. On the first day, by mutual consent, the agenda was scrapped and all the people divided into the four language groups – Spanish, Mataco, Toba and Choroti – and spent the time in prayer, asking the Lord what he was wanting to say to the Church. In the evening they all came together, to discover that all four groups had come to the same conclusion: in the coming year the emphasis should be on evangelism, and this should be backed by several half-nights of prayer. It was arranged to start these on December 31st, 1973, and so in each church in the diocese from eight o'clock till twelve that night little groups gathered, asking God to pour out his Spirit on his church.

A fortnight later, on January 14th, Pat Harris was visiting Santa Maria. He drove into the village to find crowds of people who all came up to greet him. This seemed a little unusual, and he asked what had happened. They told him how on December 31st a group of young people had been loitering together outside the village, when suddenly they felt an overwhelming sense of the presence of God, so intense that they fell to the ground. Getting up again, very frightened, they ran into the village where they saw the little flickering light of a paraffin lamp in the church.

Running into the church where the people were praying, they asked them to help them to know God. From that beginning, a movement spread throughout the village, and Pat Harris remembers that on the evening of his visit 'a service which began at eight went on until two in the morning, and it seemed like half an hour. People were coming forward to commit their lives to Christ; there was a great work of God's Spirit among them which was totally unplanned and unexpected, apart from the fact that all were praying.'

He continues:

About three or four days later, I took two people from Santa Maria with me to San Luis, where Samuel and Carlos lived. It was a terribly hot day so we went swimming, and then later in the day as it got cooler the people all came and sat round to chat, so I took the opportunity to preach a sermon. I could sense that God's Spirit was at work, so I asked if anyone wanted to say anything. A young man came forward and immediately broke down, which is most unusual for the Matacos. He began to pour out his heart about how he had turned away from God and now wanted to come back. Then the chief, a vigorous opponent of Christianity, came forward and so did many others. I left the next day, but a few months later there were forty candidates for baptism and confirmation in San Luis, a small village of about a hundred and forty people. One of them was Carlos's son José, who had been a coca addict. Pablo, the Revills' former houseboy who had been a leader in the church in Santa Maria and had then gone away from the Lord, was also touched by the Spirit of God and came right back – a great answer to our prayers. He moved to Tartagal and became a leader of the church there.

Pat Harris stayed in the Argentine Chaco for seven more years after his consecration as bishop. During the seventeen years that he had worked there altogether, he saw much growth and progress on many fronts in the work of the Church.

One question over which the missionaries had been exercised for many years was that of land rights. The land on which the Indians had lived for generations was not their own; apart from the two small areas owned by the mission at Algarrobal and San Andres, much of it was fiscal land – i.e., land owned by the state, so that Pat was able to write in 1976 that 'of the approximately sixty-five Indian villages with which we are connected, only six have land rights.'

The Indians had no security of tenure, and if any of the land were to be bought up by development companies or private landlords, they could be forced to leave. Indeed, some of the land was already owned by absentee landlords living in Buenos Aires, who up until now had shown little interest in it. However the very success of the mission's agricultural schemes was beginning to wake other people up to the fact that the land was possibly more valuable than they had thought, and this made the Indians' position more precarious.

As far back as 1964 Kevin Bewley, the missionary from Australia, and David Gonzalez from La Paz had approached the Governor of Salta about land rights for the Indians, but for years nothing was done. The problem became more urgent over the years, as with the discovery of oil near Juarez and the initial apparent success of the mission's own agricultural projects, the land was becoming more desirable. Eventually in the late 1970s it became possible for the Church to purchase land near Mision Chaqueña and the River Bermejo on behalf of the Indians, using funds solicited from aid agencies in Europe, the United States and Canada. They haven't had to leave their favourite haunts yet, but this land is there as a 'safety net' for them should they need it.

Many other things happened during Pat Harris's time as bishop. Sometimes he became involved in a particular situation where the rights of the Indians needed to be defended, as, for example, the murder case in 1976 involving four Indians from La Paz. They had been arrested and put into prison, but it was clear upon closer examination that they could not have been guilty. Pat managed to get a lawyer to act on their behalf, and also made history by persuading the judges (pointing out that they might get a few good days' shooting!) to travel from Salta to La Paz itself to hear the witnesses. As a result of the trial, the Indians were acquitted.

The material situation of the Indians fluctuated considerably during the 1970s, so that in 1975 Pat wrote that

> the critical economic situation in the country has particularly affected the Indian people. In recent years there has been steady work for a large number, cutting down hardwood trees to make fencing posts, but the bottom has dropped out of this industry, as a result of problems affecting the cattle-farming, which have in turn meant a vast drop in demand for fencing posts. Many Indians are having to return to traditional methods of hunting and fishing and generally living off the forest, but this is not easy due to diminishing game and to the fact that young people have not learned from their fathers the forest lore which is necessary for survival. And so the agricultural programme of the Mission takes on even greater significance for the people.

And in 1976 he wrote:

> I can never remember the Indians on the River Pilcomayo and other areas of the Chaco being so badly off economically. For many there is no work at all; supplies of forest animals and fish are greatly diminished and, further, many of the younger men have never been trained for a life of subsistence in the forest. They are having to learn it late in life and do not find it easy. The rate of tuberculosis is high.

The galloping inflation in Argentina affected the Indians, too, although their lives were governed less by money than most, and in 1976 while rejoicing over the printing of five thousand generously subsidised copies of the Mataco New Testament by the Argentine Bible Society, he pointed out that even so 'many of the Indian brethren are going to find it difficult to afford the price of the books.'

The work among the Spanish-speaking congregations flourished particularly. In 1976 two Argentines were ordained into the Anglican ministry at Juarez, and in Salta three new small churches were built and used as spearheads for evangelism in the rougher down-town areas. In Embarcacion, too, a Spanish-speaking church was growing, starting from the first convert in 1968. In 1975 their new church building was dedicated, and in that same year ten new members were confirmed, including a retired police sergeant who had been converted and healed through the ministry of one of the Indian pastors, Juan Barrosa.

For almost the first time in history Spanish-speaking Argentines were accepting the ministry of tribal Indian

Indian Bishop Mario Mariño crossing river Bermejo in hollowed-out bottle tree boat

people. This brings us to one of the most important events to take place at this time: the consecration of Mario Mariño as Assistant Bishop of Northern Argentina. An intelligent, reliable and humble man, he was respected as a leader and pastor. He was particularly responsible for the care of the churches near Juarez and in the Chaco province. The churches in the latter area are especially difficult to reach as the River Bermejo cuts them off – there is no bridge near at hand and there are only small ferry boats. Mario travelled by motor bike which he ferried over the river, so that he could reach these very isolated churches. When he became bishop he refused to alter his lifestyle, and remained living amongst his own people as he always had done.

In 1980 Pat and his wife Valerie had to leave Argentina – primarily because of the educational needs of their middle child, David, who had been born with minor brain damage in 1971. David Leake became bishop in Pat's stead, and two years later it became abundantly clear, as Pat himself put it, that 'God's hand was guiding us through the problems of our son.' The Falklands crisis broke, and whereas Pat as an Englishman would have been a liability to the Church in Argentina at that time, David Leake with his Argentine nationality was clearly God's man to take on the pastoring and leadership of his people. He was also, in 1983, to become the first Primate of the new Anglican Province of the Southern Cone of South America.

23
I See for Myself

July 1987: Leaving a damp summer, my family and all my usual commitments behind me, I had flown into the unknown and a grey winter morning in Buenos Aires. Emily Tompkins, daughter-in-law of Alfred Tompkins, one of the first missionaries, kindly met me and showed me the sights of Buenos Aires in her car, and after lunch she and her husband, Norman, took me to the plane for my flight north. The rain stopped and it certainly wasn't cold. I was amused to see elegant ladies in fur coats at the airport. It was winter, so they wore them!

A few hours later David and Rachel Leake met me at Salta, an ancient city built in Spanish style, set like a jewel in the north-west of the country, completely surrounded by hills. I spent two days with them there, during which time I was established in a little office in the Anglican diocesan centre – a simple, but very commodious place, with offices, storerooms, meeting rooms, a chapel, and upstairs a hostel where all sorts of people are put up for short spells. An Indian man was in one room, waiting to visit his wife who was very ill in hospital; also some American students, here on an evangelistic tour with Campus Crusade for Christ. Here, too, are kept the old mission journals, etc., which I was able to study.

David hurtles around in Salta. When not dictating letters in his office, he was buying spectacles for Indian students on the course at Mision Chaqueña who couldn't see to read; buying a guitar on behalf of another, and arranging to have short-wave radio fixed in the church's Land-Rover so he can keep in touch with the various centres while travelling. He seems very delighted about this. At home, as on their travels, David and Rachel are rarely alone, as one person after another drops in to talk.

In Salta, too, I met Helena Oliver and her mother in their comfortable house outside the town. As Rachel put it, one feels cocooned in love in their home. It's a curious experience meeting for the first time someone one has already imagined and written about. Helena has worked on various projects with the Iglesia Anglicana, and now helps her mother and teaches in a school for emotionally disturbed children. Whenever she can, she goes back to be with her friends at Santa Maria and in other parts of the Chaco. She is convinced that we have as much to learn from them as they from us.

The following day dawned cold but bright and clear. With the sun soon warming us, we set off on our travels, eastwards and northwards under a bright blue sky. The foothills of the Andes rose far away to our left, and many flowering trees were out, growing wild along the way. We drove through the area of the sugar-cane fields – San Pedro where the Leach brothers had their estate.

Then, leaving behind us the lorries stacked with thick brown sticks of cane, we went on through orange-growing country: fields of orange-trees, lemons, mangoes, bananas and castor-oil bushes. Everything was green and fertile – it seemed like the Garden of Eden to me! Soon we crossed a huge river; the Bermejo, and eventually reached the growing town of Embarcacion. By now we were in the Chaco. Embarcacion is like a set in a cowboy film: one-storey buildings lining dusty streets. Everything was dusty now – particularly the road.

Mision Chaqueña at Algarrobal, some twenty miles farther on, was just as I imagined it. A large, peaceful 'compound' with little houses all round where the students on the courses stay, and others not far away where Mataco families live. There are several big trees – some are the algarrobo which in spring become brilliantly green; also the delightful bottle-trees with swollen bottle-shaped trunks, which used to be scooped out to make boats or containers for beer. We stayed in one of the original mission houses – 'the vicarage' – where the Tompkins family lived: pleasant, bare rooms with roughly plastered walls, solid wooden furniture and an open wood fire.

It was time for the mid-week evening service soon after our arrival, so we all went. The church is just a few steps away in the middle of the mission. Built by Edward Bernau and extended by William Everitt, it is simple and dignified, with wooden columns and beams supporting the roof. The service – my first among the Indians – was very moving. There were forty to fifty people there, mostly students on the current course with their families, the children running in and out but not disturbing at all.

It was lovely singing 'O God our help in ages past' in Mataco, but good though it was, I was told later that this church is not reaching the younger people. Its leaders are too traditional – too loyal to the way the old missionaries did things, which are not all appropriate today. There has, however, been a mini-revival here recently, with people converted and coming back to the Lord, and praise-meetings and singing with guitars, but the older leaders incline to hold things back.

Afterwards we all went outside and stood around and talked. The sun was setting in an orange glow, some green parrots were screeching in a tree. Everyone shook hands and smiled and seemed glad that we were there. A crescent moon shone; smoke rose from the Indians' fires. Some children were playing marbles in the dust. It was hard to believe that I was really there, among the people about whom I had read and thought so much.

Next day David took me to visit an old pastor, Guilfredo Ibarra, whose father, Martin, was the first Indian to be converted here. Guilfredo and his wife live in a neat two-roomed house made mostly of vertical slats of wood with lots of gaps between, with a dried mud floor. They have a few pieces of good solid furniture, made on the mission, some baskets of odds and ends hanging from the ceiling, and a portable radio. Cocks and hens, dogs and cats, wander in and out.

Guilfredo knows a lot of the early history of the mission.

Most of what he told me I have already included earlier in this account. Here I just add his closing words: 'When Richard Hunt left, he embraced me. "There will be difficulties and tensions," he said, "but don't desert the word of God." Like that I was prepared. I don't fear for the Church. I see the students on the course and how faithful they are. I have told you about the beginning of the Church here. Now we see the fruit.'

After leaving Guilfredo, I went and sat in on a class which David was holding for the students on the course. In a small room with desks, one of three rooms which comprise the Bible Institute, were twelve men, some of whom had travelled a long way to be there. David was trying to help them to think about the wider issues which they encounter as Christians today. He started the discussion by reading an article from a newspaper about a young Argentine woman who has started making a name for herself by singing songs supposedly based on traditional Indian music. She blames the missionaries for suppressing this music, which was always associated with witch-doctoring. David asked the students for their views, and they all said it had nothing to do with prohibition by missionaries. The people themselves judged from their reading of the Bible what was good.

During the class, an old man behind me was writing something slowly and laboriously. I discovered later that he was Ascencio Castillo, who was recently ordained having worked faithfully as a church leader in the Las Lomitas area for over forty years. I assumed that he was taking notes, but then he read it all out, and it turned out to be a message which he handed to me. In translation, it read as follows:

We who are in Las Lomitas. I am of the Mataco Wichi tribe. ['Wichi' is the Matacos' own name for themselves.] Missionaries came to us in 1940. They told us, 'We come to you, we do not come to you with food, we do not bring you clothes, we only bring you God's words.' One called Pites [this was their name for Alfred Leake – it means 'the tall one'] knows us and the places we live in. We still continue

God's words given to us by the Anglicans. That is all for the moment. The Lord be with you. Thank you. Greetings.

After lunch, David took us a short drive to see the wooden cross which marks the spot where the first Mataco believers were baptised. This was where Mision Chaqueña used to be before it was forced to move by the flooding of the Bermejo. An inscription on the cross gives the date as April 2nd, 1922. David told us how a few days before, he had brought some of the students here. They were very moved, and one of them took a mandarin out of his pocket, saying, 'Like this fruit, we are the fruit of that first baptism.'

When we got back, the next amazing event took place. David had brought back from England a trunk full of traditional objects which his father had collected while working among the Tobas. He had decided to show them to the Indians – he is thinking of setting up an Indian museum in Juarez and was interested to hear their comments. They were certainly pleased to see them, and one or two of the men were very knowledgeable about them. There were ostrich-feather anklets, bead-work belts and bags, gourd rattles used by witch-doctors, head-dresses and trumpets for leaders in battle, little dolls made of ostrich-knuckles, humming tops, pipes, shell-necklaces, string bags and much more. David and Rachel thought some of the people seemed a bit embarrassed, or amused, or even shocked by these things – they certainly were interested. It was lovely, too, to see how the children enjoyed them and treated them with respect. They picked them up, but gently – the girls loved the necklaces and dolls.

The next day we visited Guilfredo again, and he showed us a precious possession – a photograph album with very old pictures going back almost to the beginning of the mission, which someone had given him. He also asked me to take a picture of him and his daughter outside the smart new house near-by, where I think his daughter lives. He and his family have done well: one of his grandsons, Bonifacio, is a trained nurse in the dispensary, and also owns and runs a nearby store. Two of his grand-daughters help in the school.

We then went to visit Nelida, who plays the organ in the church. (This is the only church I saw on my travels with an organ. In most they sing very well unaccompanied, and the young people sometimes lead choruses with a guitar.) Nelida is a lovely lady with a sweet smile – her father was one of the early Christians. She brought out a tin box and also showed us photographs. I was told later that she has recently been taking a strong lead in the church – starting up a women's prayer-meeting which has brought new life, and leading the meetings at the first women's conference held here at Easter.

Helena Oliver was a speaker at the conference, and the cost of the ladies' travel and food were met by the Mothers' Union in England. Another Mataco lady I met, Yolanda, is writing down her experiences with Helena Oliver's help. Yolanda led the Bible studies at the conference.

Near Nelida's house I found Alec Dean, a young Argentine Christian, with some Indians who are beginning, with his encouragement, to make exquisite carved wooden birds which he sells in the cities. He explained that it is much better economically and ecologically for them to make these, which sell very well, than to go on making the old mission chairs which use a lot of wood and are expensive and difficult to transport.

There was one missionary living at Algarrobal, Annette McCaw, from New Zealand. Trained theologically and as a nurse, she first came out to Argentina in 1966, and was involved in medical work at La Paz, Juarez and Embarcacion – including inoculation programmes and training nursing auxiliaries. Her work now is largely pastoral – helping and praying with people who come to her with problems, of which there are many. Problems in relationships, problems in health, and as Annette explained,

These are a spiritual people. Evil spirits are still very real to them, even when they are Christians, and if their children are ill they still tend to go to a witch-doctor. There is an Indian near here, Anselmo, who is supposed to have healing powers, and bus-loads of people come to him from the cities. But we try to encourage the people here to go to the doctor, and to pray to God who is stronger than the evil spirits.

This was my last day at Mision Chaqueña. Everyone was leaving: the students and their families, laden with bags of clothes from England, which Rachel and Heather had been sorting till late last night, went off in a truck to the nearest railway station. (Heather and Juan Carlos Sosa, a young Argentine couple from Salta, have been helping with the course. Among other things, Juan Carlos teaches the students Spanish choruses which they can then use in their churches.)

Also leaving was Patricia Voute, a pretty young anthropology student who was fast coming to the conclusion that what anthropologists said against missionaries was all wrong. In the afternoon we too left, heading for Tartagal. We met the students and Patricia again, still waiting in the field by the railway station for their train. Patient, philosophical and still smiling, they were to wait as things turned out until ten o'clock that night. After many handshakings, we left them, bright in their new clothes and in new head-scarves which Patricia had bought for the ladies, waving until we were out of sight.

Tartagal was quite a different experience: we stayed in a big house belonging to the Iglesia Anglicana and run by Alicia and José Sicka. Alicia mans the radio contact and provides endless hospitality; José does pastoral and social work here in the town and in the Pilcomayo villages not so far away. He is helping the Indians with a cotton-growing project, and bales of it were in his yard. There seemed to be an awful lot of people in the house: in particular the Campus Crusade students, just back from a foray to the Pilcomayo villages, where they had shown the 'Jesus film' and got covered with dust. Many young people in the villages had enjoyed the film.

Next day we set off again, this time for Santa Maria, the first of the Pilcomayo villages and the place where my story began. The drive, though bumpy, was beautiful, with mimosa and prickly pear growing beside the road. Santa Maria is a small and peaceful Indian village, very green, with neat wooden huts scattered among the trees.

The government project which first took Helena there had soon folded up, and Helena herself left the government service. However, with the help of some French Catholics she had continued to help the people, enabling them to get corrugated roofing and a well. We were warmly greeted by Zebedeo, the pastor, who opened up Helena's house for us and brought chairs, a table, two beds and wood for a fire.

Soon we were sitting outside, boiling a kettle on the fire to make some tea. The teapot we had with us, incidentally, was a small metal one, showing signs of Alfred's clever improvisations, which Alfred and Dorothy Leake had used years before at the Toba mission. Some women outside another house were cooking several large fish from the river. They had propped them on sticks, cone-shaped all round the fire. It was a wonderful sight, with cats, dogs, pigs and children all gathered around, scavenging where they could. Soon some of the fish was brought over to us and we ate it with our fingers for our supper. It was good.

The sun set, the moon and the stars came out and the people still sat beside their fires. Dogs barked and the occasional child shouted or cried. As David sat by our fire he was never alone. Now one, now another of the men of the village would come to sit and talk to him while he listened, nodding, poking the fire, occasionally throwing in a word. One old Christian man was telling him how worried he is about his son, an ordained pastor who has gone right away from God. The pastors are not paid, so they need other work. This young man got a government post in a nearby school, but the money he earned led him to drinking and to leaving his wife for other girls. It is a pattern all too easy to follow. Poverty is certainly bad, but even relative affluence can all too easily lead people away from God.

I slept, still finding it hard to believe that I was really there, with Rachel and Judith her daughter in Helena's one-roomed hut. We had two beds. Rachel and Judith shared one of them. David spent the night in the Land-Rover. Sometimes the dogs seemed to go mad and bedlam reigned, but generally I had a very good night.

Next day there was a communion service (1662 in Mataco!) in the packed church, led by David in his white surplice with its two red bands over his jeans and sweater, and Zebedeo – his surplice with two black bands. David preached on Romans 8. He described a dream in which Rachel had rung him from England and said only these five words: 'Someone wants to destroy you.' For a time he was always on the look-out for danger. Then one day, as he was talking to a Toba Christian about this – for these people are experienced in dreams – the man said, 'No, David, I don't think it is anything to do with you personally. But Satan is wanting to destroy the church.' David went on to show how insidiously this can happen – rather as in the sad case of the young pastor. But Romans 8 tells us that God is stronger than evil, and will not allow his church to be destroyed. At the end of the service, for about two minutes everyone prayed spontaneously and simultaneously – quite something! They aren't so shy that way. The church is the focal point of nearly every village we visited.

An interesting observation has been made by J. H. Palmer in his thesis, where he points out that for the Matacos and Tobas, the church service has replaced the dance as the major communal activity, serving, among other things, as an act of solidarity. After church a lorry from Tartagal drove into the village and collected a whole lot of men who rushed out with their fishing nets. The fish they caught would be taken back to Tartagal to be sold. We visited a girl in bed with TB, and prayed with her and her family.

Eventually we left, taking a pregnant girl to hospital on the way. The road was very dusty and deeply rutted. It was also exceedingly hot. We passed through several Indian villages, and wherever we stopped, people came out to shake us by the hand. At last we reached La Paz, and here a large crowd came out to greet us: Chunupis, Chorotis and Matacos all live here. We stayed in Mr and Mrs Dickson's old house, now empty, on the site of the house which George Revill built for his family. The Argentine doctor and his wife who now run the clinic which Michael Patterson set up, invited us in for a welcome cup of tea.

La Paz is a large village, fortunate in having been able to remain on its original river-bank site. The Pilcomayo seen at last, as Bishop Every said! It was sunset and very beautiful. Although comparatively empty at this time of the year, it is still a very big river, the banks here sandy and bordered with thick trees. On the other side is Paraguay. I talked to Felipe Gonzalez, the pastor at La Paz, in his little office full of papers and files. He told me:

> This place used to be called *Nopok-wet*, 'the dammed-up river'. My grandfather, Alfredo Gonzalez, lived here, where the carpenter's shop now is. He was a witch-doctor who had two sons, David and Lucas. The people used to dance in those days, and one day the two boys went for the dancing to Santa Maria. On their second night there, they heard George Revill preach, and they went back and told their father, 'There's a man there who is talking about different things – about God who exists from ancient times.'
>
> 'Go back and listen again,' their father said. So they did. Finally their father said, 'Go back and tell him that if he wants to come here, it would be good.' When George Revill heard this, he replied, 'If you help me make a raft, I'll come downstream.' So they floated him down the river and he built an adobe house for his family and settled here. My grandfather left drinking and witchcraft and told his sons to do the same. My father David and his brother Lucas, with George Revill, founded this church.
>
> David Gonzalez was one of the first seven Matacos to be ordained. I made a pact with him that I wouldn't leave the church. I went to the Bible Institute at Algarrobal, completing my primary education there as well; I did exten-

River Pilcomayo at La Paz.

sion courses in agriculture and mechanics, and Pat Harris taught me to play the accordion and the guitar. I have done a lot of work with musical groups, and then I was ordained and became the pastor here.

Felipe is impressively energetic and seems to get things done. This, with his musical gifts, means that the young people are coming to his church, as we saw next morning when over thirty people, mostly young, were confirmed by David Leake. There is another pastor here, Julian Gomez, who is also a gifted musician and has written some simplified Bible-story books in Wichi. He is a Choroti, and the Gonzalez family are partly Choroti as well. Difficulty between tribal groups often surfaces in the life of the church – as today, when it gave rise to some uncertainty during the service as to who exactly was meant to be being confirmed!

Our departure for Tartagal was delayed as David got involved in trying to settle a dispute about corrugated iron roofing for someone's house. At Pozo Tigré where we stopped, one old man thought I was Mrs Revill; they all remember her with great affection. There was trouble here when an Indian helping to rebuild the church as part of the social project went off with the pastor's daughter, taking the pastor and the corrugated iron for the church with him. So the poor people of Pozo Tigré now have no pastor and no church. They seemed very pleased to be visited, and all prayed the Lord's Prayer in Wichi.

At Tartagal it was marvellous to wash all the Chaco dust out of our hair, and next day we drove – a long, hot dusty drive – to Juarez.

24
Sorties from Juarez

At Juarez, David and Rachel stayed in their old house where they had lived from 1963 to 1972. I stayed with Helen Sohns, a missionary who told me she had trained as a nurse in Germany and in England, and had come out to the Chaco in 1958. At that time Barbara Kitchen was the only single lady missionary there, and she needed company. Also there was no nurse at all in the mission, so Helen's prayer for an 'open door' was decisively answered.

Her first placement was Pozo Yacaré, and she and Barbara set off in a mule-cart. They had just arrived when a severe whooping-cough epidemic broke out. With no antibiotics as yet to help fight infections, about twenty children died – not an encouraging start, and poor Helen felt like going straight home. However, she set up a little dispensary, and for the next two years she and Barbara travelled between Pozo Yacaré and San Patricio, running both missions. They did everything, including running the store, the profits from which were needed for the medicines they used.

They were the last resident missionaries there, as in the 1960s the new mission policy of the three main centres began. Helen then went to La Paz, and as we have seen, was already nursing and running the dispensary there when the Pattersons arrived. She began training Indians to give injections out of necessity; as the only nurse in the Argentine Chaco, she had to have help. At first they were volunteers, but later some got their 7th grade primary education and then did a government course which qualified them for paid government posts in the villages where they lived. Helen herself was a tutor on a special course for Indians at Tartagal.

After four months' enforced exile in Paraguay at the time of the Falklands War, Helen, being a much-needed nurse, was asked to go back to Argentina. She now trains Indian women to be midwives and to give antenatal care in their own communities.

A cold south wind blew up overnight and the next day was grey and wintry. I interviewed Bishop Mario in the diocesan office, as already described. He explained to me how for Indians in the towns, life is complex – much more so than it used to be in their tranquil forest life. He sees his own job, particularly, as counselling and helping the Indian pastors so that they in turn can teach and counsel the people. 'Training is also important,' he continued. 'We must emphasise what the Bible says; and we must also apply the richness of the Word of God to the situations which people face. The Church must speak with a prophetic voice, as God's prophets did long ago.'

We went on a long day trip visiting various Indian communities. At Pozo Maza we found some of the exceptionally ragged and poor-looking people who used to live at Carmen. I felt sorry for them in the bitter wind. Next, at Vaca Perdida we found a delightful Toba community where everyone was bright and smiling and well-dressed. These people used to live upriver from Mision El Toba, and their dispensary (which they offered to us for eating our lunch in) bore the legend: '*Esta botica fue donado a la mision el Toba por the East Runton Missionary Association*'.[20]

We then went on to Rinconada – the place where the Tobas from MET moved when Sombrero Negro was flooded. Here we met an old man – Modesto – who used to drive the cart for Alfred Leake. Venerated in the tribe, he gave me an audience, with a small crowd gathered round, and told us how he became a Christian. Before our interview began, he insisted on bringing out the chair – which he sat in – and a large water jug, significant because it used to belong to Alfred and Dorothy Leake. Apparently one day Bill Price, one of the missionaries, said to him, 'I look for you on Sundays, but I don't see you in church. Would you come if you had a shirt?' He thought he would, so a shirt was found and Modesto started going to church. And, as his aged wife added, 'He used to be very difficult, but from that time he went forward – he didn't let go.'

Modesto either remembers or heard from his father how 'the settlers used to accuse us of stealing cattle so they could arrest us and kill us. We used to kill the soldiers and take the gold out of their teeth. We would catch one and scalp him while he was still alive.'

The day we met Modesto at Rinconada, the Tobas heard over their radio that the land on which they live is being handed over to them on August 15th this year. (Many villages have a radio system with their own aerial now; something the provincial government has provided to enable them to get emergency medical help.) This handing-over of the land is something for which the Iglesia Anglicana has been pressing for a long time. Presumably it is being done now in the hope of catching the Indians' votes in the elections on September 6th, but it's a good thing none the less.

Next day I spent the morning talking to some of the missionaries at Juarez – first to Bob and Margaret Lunt, who are living in David and Rachel's old house (the house, incidentally, where when Bob and Margaret leave, David hopes to house the Wichi museum). First Margaret told me how from the time when, at the age of 12, she had woken suddenly in the night with a real sense of God's holiness and the need to turn to Christ for forgiveness, she had been led to study medicine. She had eventually landed up at La Paz, the only doctor from Crevo to Juarez, often travelling long distances by bicycle to visit her patients.

Bob on the other hand was converted at Nottingham University where he was studying Spanish. He trained in librarianship and then, hearing of a long-standing need for a linguist in Northern Argentina who could work on a new Mataco version of the New Testament, he did a course in linguistics and went out to Mision Chaqueña.

Bob and Margaret met in the Chaco, and, once married, they eventually settled in Tartagal. Bob had met the Indian, Isidro Vilte, who he felt was the one to help him in the translation work, and they had completed twenty-seven of

the 260 chapters of the New Testament when the Falklands
crisis broke in 1982. The diocese gave them overnight notice
to leave. Then followed nine nightmarish days when, with a
seriously ill child, they attempted to leave via Bolivia but,
baulked by torrential rain, eventually got away from Salta
and reached safety in Asuncion, Paraguay.

From there they went to England and thought they probably wouldn't go back. However, after two years any bitter-
ness and doubt they felt was dissipated by some Argentine
Christians they met at a conference, and it became clear to
them that they should return and that Bob should complete
the translation. (At a time when Argentine visas were hard to
get, the fact that their daughter Elizabeth was Argentine
saved the day!)

This time they moved to Juarez, where Isidro now lived.
This is how Bob described their meeting on their return:

Two Mataco Indians and I stop once more in the tracks of
our struggle to move a refrigerator across the mission
compound in Juarez. Weary, we look around for assist-
ance, when our eyes behold an awesome sight. At the gate,
dismounting from his bicycle, gaze fixed straight and
determined, imposingly strong, stands Isidro Vilte, co-
translator of the Mataco New Testament and now, for
three minutes of his distinguished and controversial
career, furniture removal supervisor and executor. Needless to say, the situation is saved. 'I just called by to see if
you'd got to Juarez yet? How are you settling in here?
Whichever day you're ready, we'll start work.' We were
moving here because a variety of reasons had led Isidro,
months ago, to move himself and all his household to the
lower shores of the River Pilcomayo, his ancestral home,
only fifty miles from Juarez – no distance at all in this
wilderness and now that oil has been found in the area
(Juarez: Boom City), an easy route for lifts.

There's also an aeroplane on which I can visit you
sometimes,' announces our hero, cycling off into the sunset
with a promise to return for the first of our work sessions

next week, while the two erstwhile fridge-removers listen stupefied.

Bob explained to me the thinking behind the new translation. The first Mataco translation was the British and Foreign Bible Society's tentative edition of Mark's Gospel translated by Richard Hunt in 1919. Then between 1919 and 1962, various separate books were translated locally, and in 1962 the Bible Society published a complete New Testament, translated by Henry Grubb and Alberto Gonzalez of San Andres. (Alberto was no relation of the Gonzalez family at La Paz, but he was, curiously enough, related to Isidro Vilte, in that Isidro's sister Isabelle was his sister-in-law. Alberto was one of Henry Grubb's best pupils. An outstanding and saintly man, his death is still commemorated in a service every year, as a sign of the love and respect which he inspired.)

Finally, in 1971, selections from the Old Testament had been translated by Maurice Jones at Algarrobal, with help from various Indians. However, the church soon realised that there was a need for a popular version (something like the Good News Bible) to be made, using a new translation method known as Dynamic Equivalence.[21] Previously, the Bible Society had insisted on a literal translation using the old method known as Formal Correspondence. Whereas a literal translation reproduces the *form* of the original Greek – a noun by a noun, etc. – Dynamic Equivalence tries to translate the *meaning* while maintaining accuracy. Thus shorter sentences and the grammar which is natural to the particular language can be used.

Margaret Lunt, too, is by no means idle, although for the moment she is not doing medical work. Soon after their return, she went on a visit to Santa Teresa and noticed that the children there weren't learning choruses any more, and had no Sunday school. Since then, as well as looking after her own two little girls, she has been doing all she can to revive the Sunday schools, producing teaching materials for all the villages single-handed.

The other missionary I spoke to was Beryl Gilbert. She is a nurse who went out to the Chaco in 1961. Based now in the hospital in Juarez, she does TB work, and is currently training primary health-care workers to do sputum tests. Now that the people she has trained are able to take some of the TB work off her shoulders, she has taken on an extra task – that of co-ordinator and distributor for the SEAN extension training.

The story of SEAN is a tale in itself. Originally standing for Seminario por Extension Argentina Norte, and created by a missionary called Tony Barrett in his home in Tucuman, it is now used worldwide as Study by Extension to All Nations. The idea is to try to have a tutor in each village church.

Beryl trains the tutors here and circulates the material. Groups of seven or eight students then take a year over the course, doing one lesson a week with a test and a discussion class at the end of each week. As a result, they are better equipped to serve God wherever they are.

In the afternoon we visited El Potrillo, fifty miles or so away. A few years ago the people from Yuto, San Andres and Pozo Algarrobo moved near-by because the Pilcomayo kept flooding and changing its course. Apparently the lovely church at San Andres, 'the cathedral of the Chaco', and that at Yuto, too, are, since severe flooding in 1986, now almost completely submerged in silt. At the place they moved to (then called El Potrillo), a Roman Catholic priest, Padre Francisco, was organising a project which gave them work: making wooden posts and railway sleepers. He also set up a school and a hospital run by nuns.

But in 1986 the whole place was destroyed by the river, so the already-mixed community plus some others moved yet again, to the place now known as El Potrillo, which is near the oil perforations and therefore already had an infrastructure of roads, an air-strip, water brought by lorry from the river, etc. It's a curious place, with several schools and churches, and indeed whole communities which have come from other places, strung out along both sides of the road. The people don't like it very much – they miss the river.

We stopped at the house of the pastor, Felipe Gutierez. He had been on the course at Algarrobal. As usual, people came out from everywhere and shook us by the hand. Then Felipe himself turned up, with Bishop Mario and various other people. They had come from Juarez in a lorry to collect some women who were going to a women's conference in Juarez. Within minutes the church bell was rung (it hung from a tree and although bell-shaped was apparently designed for closing off an oil-pipe), and we all gathered in the new half-built church for a service. Most of these people originally came from Yuto. The other pastor is Noé, who was pastor when Mr and Mrs Panter were there. Bishop Mario preached, saying among other things that there is so much uncertainty today, so many ways we can go, but the only lasting truth is in Christ, the Way, the Truth and the Life. Only he can meet our deepest needs.

After the service I met an old lady, Juana, who used to help Mrs Panter in the kitchen and whose husband was an evangelist. She said that the newer missionaries aren't the same as the old ones used to be. 'They lived with us and shared our lives. These new ones come and shake us by the hand and go away again. These are the white man's ways.' (This, I am sure, was no criticism of individuals, but an old person's reaction to new ways of doing things: 'Things aren't what they were . . .')

I have enjoyed watching the children in these villages. Up to 2 years old or more, they are carried in a sling by their mother, in such a position that they can suckle at any time. Older children play in groups – usually a little gang of girls or of boys together. They all seem very happy and co-operate well. They have very few toys.

Next day, before leaving Juarez, we went to the diocesan centre where the women's conference was in progress. It was all very well organised, with hymn and chorus sheets, programmes, speakers and the theme 'As for me and my house, we will serve the Lord.' The Indians love courses and conferences and put up with considerable discomfort to get to them. Here were some ladies I had met before – Nelida from

Algarrobal and others. Also just before we left, I was happy
to meet Isabelle Vilte – sister of Isidro and a nurse in the
hospital at Juarez – who is a leader in the Juarez church. Well
past midnight, after a nine-hour drive, we reached Salta
which we had left ten days before.

Back in Salta, on Sunday, we went to San Andres – a lively, growing church, growing so fast that it is having to rebuild. The day we went they were rejoicing in a gift from England, large enough, helped by the favourable exchange rate, to enable them to complete the ceiling of the new church.

From talking to various people I have tried to piece together the story of the growth of the *Iglesia Anglicana* among the Spanish-speaking townspeople. I shall describe particularly developments in Salta, but in Juarez, Embarcacion, Tartagal and other towns, similar developments have taken place.

Joyce Illingworth, whom I met in Buenos Aires on my way back to England, told me part of the story. She first went to Salta in 1967 where she found a very small leadership team and a very small church. Bill Flagg was there with his wife Marjorie, he at that time archdeacon and area superintendent for SAMS. Valerie Pilbrow, later to become Valerie Harris, was working as his secretary. It had recently been decided to move the headquarters of the Anglican church from Embarcacion to Salta. The church possessed only two houses, and they housed not only people but the office and the church services as well. Joyce helped with administration and book-keeping; she also began arranging children's meetings.

In 1968 Maurice and Gill Sinclair came to Salta for language study and with hopes of church planting. Maurice began teaching English at the university, and this gave him contact with the students. Small church meetings were held in the Sinclairs' garage. By the time Joyce returned from her first leave in England in 1972, Maurice himself had become primarily involved in the Chaco agricultural project.

However two more young couples eager to encourage church growth had arrived in Salta: Walter and Sally Robbins and Glyn and Jane Jones, and a new thrust forward began for the Church.

Meetings were held in various homes, and in 1974 it was decided that they could no longer continue meeting in rented property, people's garages and front rooms, so prefabricated buildings were bought. These were erected in two different places on the outskirts of Salta and became the first two local churches there: one in a suburb called Tres Cerritos, the other at Don Ceferino. At that time, too, the church administration moved into a new office building which had been bought in the centre of town. It had also a store-room, a shop, and a chapel where services were started which tended to attract professional people – the congregation which eventually became the church of San Andres. The idea of the shop was to sell craft-work made by the Indians in the Chaco.

With the growth of the Chaco agricultural project during the 1970s, large sums of money were coming into the diocese, so an accountant, David Dixie, was appointed. Joyce, freed from book-keeping, concentrated on developing Sunday-school work in the Chaco and in the towns, both by preparing material and by training teachers. She also continued her involvement with various church groups, even pastoring the church at Ceferino for a year, and helping Stephen Barrett with theological education.

Joyce was the one English person who managed to delay her departure at the time of the Falklands crisis just long enough until the pressure was off, and in the end she never left at all. Her dark hair and Latin features and excellent Spanish helped as well. However it was an unsettling time, and soon afterwards she left Salta and went to live in Buenos Aires, becoming involved in pastoral counselling there. There are now several Anglican congregations in Salta, one of which meets in the local prison, and some in very poor shanty-town areas on the outskirts, where most people live in tiny one-roomed shacks with no proper sanitation and consequently in very poor health.

So, what is the situation in the *Iglesia Anglicana* now, and how to sum up our story? The situation, of course, is always changing. Undeniably the powerful all-pervasive Western secular culture has invaded the world of the Chaco Indians. The white man's store, the transistor radio, the police post, the fish lorries, the flying doctor, the oil installations and much more are all heralds of the sophisticated, competitive, commercialised West. The Indian has to absorb and adapt to all this change within a generation – it is the resultant anxiety that brings the Indians flocking round David and Rachel Leake when they visit.

As we have seen, education programmes and health education schemes run by the church all aim to help, as do the agricultural projects. These latter have been scaled down considerably to small economic schemes which relate directly to the Indians' natural life style. In recent years some painful re-appraisal has even taken place in the hearts and minds of Christians as to how far they are right to impose development schemes at all upon the Indians' way of life: 'For them, living is more important than personal achievement and advancement. We do not want, through rigid projects, to introduce them to all the tensions and frustrations of our materialistic lives . . .'[22]

A balance must be found. We want to help and to show our love in practical form, but it must be done in the right way. Undoubtedly, too, the Argentine government is doing much more for the Indians now, and rightly so. In the church scene also much has changed. In particular, the withdrawal of missionaries at the time of the Falklands war has accelerated the nationalising of the Anglican Church in Argentina, so that leadership is now in the hands of Argentines, both Indian and white. There are also hopeful signs of increasing co-operation with the Roman Catholic Church.

As we bring this simple history to an end, let us listen to a few final comments. First, J. H. Palmer again, the researcher:

SAMS missionary work was begun at a time of rapid expansion of the national frontier society and consequent white/Indian antagonism, against which the Anglican missionary protected the Mataco. The 'kind' words of the Bible and the 'kind' acts of its spokesmen corresponded to Mataco ideals of behaviour. Also missionary policy has consistently balanced a concern for the spiritual welfare of the Mataco with a concern for their social welfare. Missionary practice among the Matacos is humanitarian and, in the context of the national society, indispensable.[23]

Second, the experience of Tricia Munday is illuminating: A nurse, she went out to Argentina with Rob, her dentist husband, in 1975 and they worked at La Paz for six years. In fact, particularly from the time her first child was born, Tricia suffered from constant ill-health, exhaustion and anxiety. She recounts how

the Indian women would come and pray for me and encourage me. All my 'Englishness' was stripped away. I was just a young mother with no granny to turn to. The Indians saw us as their responsibility. 'Goodness me,' they must have thought, 'here comes another young couple. We must help them.' Very graciously, they would keep an eye on me, especially when Rob was away.

Finally, as our story began with Helena, it seems fitting that it should end with her. This is what she said to me shortly before I left Salta:

It was God's loving purpose to bring me to Santa Maria when he did. He was already speaking to me. I wasn't looking for God, but God was looking for me. In the same way, he was reaching out to the Indians even before the missionaries came. Jesus told us not to be anxious about food, drink and clothes, but to learn from his loving provision for the birds and his clothing of the flowers. They do not worry, but God provides for them. We should trust him too.

But this lesson the Indians already know. They have no

money, no salary, but they have been living this teaching out in practice for centuries. Certain truths he revealed to them, but the fulness of the Gospel was brought to them by the missionaries, and then through them, to me. God's plan is *one* – it is a whole plan. It's not one person's plan, or a missionary society's plan; it's not for one period of history only. God's love embraces us, and we find ourselves brothers and sisters. This is his plan, and it is for his glory.'

Praise him.

Indian girl carrying water-pot.

Notes

1 Father Alejano M Corrado, *El Colegio Franciscano de Tarija*, 1884
2 Marsh and Stirling, *The Story of Allen Gardiner* (London 1878), p 35
3 For more about the remarkable life and death of Allen Gardiner, see Phyllis Thompson, *An Unquenchable Flame* (Hodder & Stoughton, 1983)
4 Frederick C MacDonald, *Bishop Stirling of the Falklands* (Seeley, Service and Co Ltd, London 1929), p 93
5 Ibid, p 138
6 W Barbrooke Grubb, *An Unknown People in an Unknown Land* (Seeley, Service and Co Ltd, 1910), p 18
7 Ibid, p 18
8 Ibid, p 323
9 The Revd R J Hunt, *The Livingstone of South America* (Seeley, Service and Co Ltd, 1932), p 262
10 Ibid, p 287
11 Ibid, p 317
12 E F Every, *South American Memories of Thirty Years* (SPCK, London, 1933), p 116
13 Alfred Metraux, *Ethnography of the Chaco – Handbook of South American Indians vol I* ed Julian H Steward, New York, 1963
14 R J Hunt, *The Matacos of the Gran Chaco* – SAMS Annual Report, 1925
15 R J Hunt, *The Livingstone of South America*, p 328–9
16 Winifred Revill, *Chaco Chapters* (Hodder & Stoughton, 1947), p 93
17 SAMS Annual Report, 1941
18 W D Reyburn, *The Toba Indians of the Argentine Chaco – an interpretive report* (1954)

19 Canon Harry Sutton, *You'll Never Walk Alone* (Marshalls Paperback, 1984), p 99

20 Translation: 'This dispensary was given to Mision El Toba by the East Runton Missionary Association.'

21 Dynamic Equivalence: Quality of a translation in which the message of the original text has been so transported into the receptor language that the response of the reader is essentially like that of the original readers. Frequently the form of the original text has to be changed to achieve this.

22 Peter Tyson, SAMS SHARE magazine, 1986

23 J H Palmer, thesis, p 91

Bibliography

Crawley, Eduardo, *A House Divided; Argentina 1880–1980* (C Hurst & Co, 1984)

Grubb, H C, *The Land Between the Rivers* (Lutterworth, 1965)

Grubb, W Barbrooke, *A Church in the Wilds* (Seeley, Service & Co, 1914)

Lewis, Norman, *The Missionaries* (Secker & Warburg, 1988)

Mann, Wendy, *An Unquenched Flame* (SAMS, 1968)

Sinclair, Maurice, *Green Finger of God* (Paternoster Press, 1980)

Slessor, Malcolm, *The Discovery of South America* (Hamlyn, 1970)